David Davies was a member of ~~~~~~~~~~
World War II. A retired chartered ~~~~~~~~~
a great interest in military and naval history, especially of the
Revolutionary and Napoleonic period. A member of the Navy
Records Society and Society for Nautical Research, for many
years he has owned and sailed a traditional gaff rigged ex-
working boat.

Praise for *Fighting Ships*
'. . . action packed with many of the great sea battles that form
such an important part of the national's history . . .'
The Nautical Magazine

'Intelligently written and informative enough to warrant a place
on even the most landlocked bookcase.' *First Empire*

A BRIEF HISTORY OF
FIGHTING
SHIPS

David Davies

CARROLL & GRAF PUBLISHERS
New York

Carroll & Graf Publishers
An imprint of Avalon Publishing Group, Inc.
161 William Street
New York
NY 10038 2607
www.carrollandgraf.com

First published in the UK as *Fighting Ships*,
by Constable and Co. Ltd, 1996

This edition published in paperback in the UK by Robinson,
an imprint of Constable & Robinson Ltd, 2002

First Carroll & Graf edition, 2002

ISBN 0–7867–0988–X

Printed and bound in the EU

Library in Congress Cataloguing-in-Publication Data is available on file.

Contents

Plates

Rear-Admiral Horatio Nelson by Lemuel Francis Abbott
(*National Maritime Museum London*)
Victory, 1765 (*National Maritime Museum London*)
Nelson's flagships at anchor by Nicholas Pocock
(*National Maritime Museum London*)
The Battle of Cape St Vincent, 14 February 1797 by
Robert Cleveley (*National Maritime Museum London*)
The Battle of the Nile, 1 August 1798 by Matthew
Nicolas Condy (*National Maritime Museum London*)
The Battle of Copenhagen, 2 April 1801 by Robert Dodd
(*National Maritime Museum London*)
Cut-away hull drawing of HMS *Victory* (*The Ministry
of Defence*)
Slung hammocks on the Lower Gundeck of HMS *Victory*
(*Pitkin Pictorials Ltd*)

Figures

Maps

Diagrams

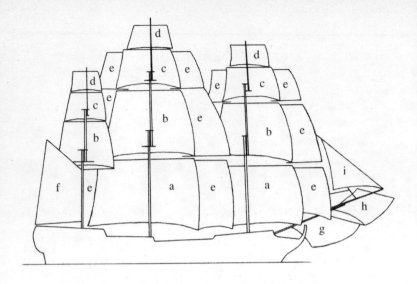

OUTLINE SKETCH OF 74 GUN SHIP
INDICATING SAILS CARRIED IN FAIR CONDITIONS
Rigging and controlling lines not shown

a. Courses
b. Topsails
c. Topgallant Sails
d. Royals
e. Studding Sails

f. Spanker
g. Spritsail
h. Spritsail Topsail
i. Flying Jib
   (other foresails concealed
   by foremast square sails)

Note on the Text

In this book I have followed the example of the late James Henderson (author of *Sloops and Brigs* and *The Frigates*) in a number of ways. The term 'larboard' for the left side of a ship has been used because this was the term in use during the period of the book and it appears in all contemporary logs and accounts. ('Larboard' was superseded by 'port' during the first half of the nineteenth century.) Similarly, old compass notations have been used – e.g., ENE instead of 67.5 degrees, and fathoms and feet are used instead of metres.

The diagrams illustrating fleet actions aim to be accurate in the general impression they give, not in every detail. For example, the number of ship symbols used in illustrating fleet movements should not be taken as necessarily the *precise* number of ships involved; and where the name of a ship is given against a symbol, the general impression of its situation is correct rather than its *exact* location. Most of this sort of information came, originally, from ships' logs; and in battle the master, responsible for the log, had a great many other things to think about. It would not be surprising if he had not the time to check and record every little variation in the direction of the ship or the wind.

The meanings of the nautical terms used in the text are mostly self-evident; a glossary of such terms is included at the end of the book if further explanation is needed.

My sincere thanks are due to a number of people who gave me help and encouragement: my family, who had to read drafts and put up with all the trauma – especially my son who checked out the times and distances involved in certain manoeuvres in the largest sailing trimaran in the world of which, at the time, he was the skipper; my friends Jan Uphill, who typed it and made encouraging remarks,

Auriol Chandler who advised me on French usages, Tony Leach, who helped me with technical and professional advice; and the staffs of the Public Record Office and the National Maritime Museum, also of the Museo Naval, Madrid. If, as is probable, there are, in spite of all this help, mistakes in the book they are my own.

Above all, my thanks are due to my friend Jeremy Howard-Williams (author of *Sails*, *Night Intruder* and many other books), whose brainchild this book is. I would not have thought for a moment of attempting to write it if he had not persuaded me to do so. Once I had started, he gave me steady encouragement and advice at all stages. He died the day before I learned that it was to be published and it is to him that it is dedicated.

CHAPTER 1

The Original World War

1793–1815 was the period of the Napoleonic wars – a loose description of a struggle which arose out of the French Revolution of 1789 and continued as resistance, by many nations, to Napoleon's attempt to impose a single monarchical government upon the whole of Europe and beyond. The struggle involved, at one time or another, most of the developed nations of the world and, if only out of respect for the peoples who endured and suffered for so long, the great wars of the twentieth century might well be called World Wars II and III.

The conflict was the last major one in which sailing ships of the line were engaged and, because of the scale of events, forms the background to their greatest achievements. This book is about the ships and not the history of the times, but to set their activities in perspective it is worth looking, very briefly, at the broad outline of the events in which they played their part.

Britain was at war with France for the whole of the period, with a brief period of uneasy peace after the Treaty of Amiens in 1802; hence the use of the plural 'wars' rather than 'war'. During the first of these wars (more precisely known as the Revolutionary war) Napoleon rose from artillery captain to become the leader of the French Republic; in the second he became emperor and the most famous Frenchman of all time. Thus Napoleonic wars.

The main protagonists were France, Austria (then much more powerful than today), Russia, Spain, Poland, Prussia and Great Britain. There were many other smaller states and principalities involved. All, with the exception of Great Britain, were, at times, enforced allies of France; they all fought against her again when opportunity offered. For the first nineteen years the pattern was, with occasional setbacks, one of continuing successful campaigns by the armies of France. They enlarged her territories until they embraced nearly the whole of Europe. At different times, different combinations or coalitions of powers offered resistance; but they all suffered eventual defeat. The major break in the pattern came in 1812, when Napoleon attacked Russia. As Hitler found some 130 years later, the weather was too hostile and the problem of supply over vast distances was too great. Having reached Moscow, Napoleon was forced to retreat and, in two terrible months, half a million men of the once glittering and triumphant Grande Armée of the French Empire died miserably in the Russian snow.

For two more years Napoleon held on, but his great days were over. Wellington's army in Spain, which had grimly held its foothold there for four years, began a remorseless advance to the Pyrenees and beyond. Subjugated countries in central and northern Europe took fresh heart and attacked from the east. In 1814 Napoleon abdicated.

About a year later, while a peace conference was in progress in Vienna, Napoleon escaped from exile in Elba and re-established himself as emperor. In an amazing display of brisk organisation, he got together a substantial and enthusiastic army; it was, however, narrowly but conclusively beaten at Waterloo on 18 June 1815, and the Napoleonic wars were over.

Of all the causes of Napoleon's eventful downfall, none was of greater significance than the Royal Navy. The British were suspicious of military power; in 1793 their army was small, ill-equipped and, like all established armies of the time, out of date. But because of the worldwide nature of Britain's trade, her navy had always been maintained at an adequate level, and was potentially more powerful than any other. Initially it was not as efficient as it became later, and errors were made; but with the emergence of admirals of the calibre of Jervis and Nelson, and a better understanding in high places of the needs of total war, it became formidable and then supreme. Its task was the same as it was to be in the wars of the twentieth century – to keep open Britain's trade routes, to carry the war to distant and vulnerable parts of the enemy's territory, and to deny the enemy the use of the sea. This was achieved by methods which may be very broadly divided under two headings: defeating enemy ships or fleets at sea; and preventing the enemy from getting to sea at all – blockade. All the activities described in the following chapters fall under one or the other of these headings.

The Royal Navy was greatly assisted by the grievous harm which had befallen the French navy at the hands of the revolutionary leaders. The old French navy had been officered by aristocrats, and by 1793 most of them had gone to the guillotine or had fled the country. No rational steps were taken to replace them with properly trained men. The fatuous doctrine was expounded that sea experience was not necessary because revolutionary fervour would offset any lack of skill; if this suggestion could apply anywhere it certainly could not apply to the very complex business of handling a big sailing ship in battle. This perverse outlook was, perhaps, assisted by the traditional feeling in a country with extensive land frontiers – that the navy was not so important as the army. The army captured territory and defeated threatening forces; the main function of the navy was to assist the army when need arose. This thinking led to such ill-advised actions as taking gunners from the ships to serve in the artillery. Napoleon, although not responsible for these revolutionary blunders, did little to correct them. He had no feeling for the sea, and could never understand that the forces of nature prevented ships from being moved freely about, as and when required, like army regiments.

In spite of these self-inflicted handicaps, and in the face of a formidable British navy, the French acquitted themselves extraordinarily well. Undertrained revolutionary fervour and patriotism could not give them victory in battle, but it did provide them with tenacity in the face of bitter and bloody defeats. Very few actions were a walkover; the Glorious First of June was a strategic victory for the French; at the Nile the doomed crews fought doggedly to the bitter end; and at Trafalgar, a scratch fleet sailed out of Cadiz to meet Nelson knowing that, short of a miracle, it was going to its destruction. But all their courage could not compensate for their lack of sea time and after a shaky start the British navy, in its sea-keeping, ship-handling and gunnery, established an ascendancy which was to prove conclusive.

CHAPTER 2

The Ships

The line of battle was a concept of naval tactics which held sway between the middle of the seventeenth century and the first half of the nineteenth. It could be briefly described as an indian file of powerful warships sailing (or in exceptional cases at anchor) one behind the other, which could be expected to fight successfully any comparable number of ships which the enemy could produce.

A ship of the line was a ship sufficiently large and sufficiently well-armed to take a place in the line of battle. It could also be known as a line-of-battle ship which became shortened to battleship – a term still in use today (1995).

The line, as a tactical formation, developed with the increasing use of big guns in warships. The practice of installing heavy guns in ships intended primarily for use in war grew during the fifteenth and sixteenth centuries, but for a long time was considered of doubtful value. The established method of sea fighting, was to lie close along-side the enemy while soldiers, not concerned in the handling of the ships, fought hand-to-hand battles. The early armed ships had large fore- and stern-castles, carrying a great many small-calibre guns, having a wide field of fire and able to give support to infantry boarding an enemy ship or defending their own vessel from boarding. A great many of the Spanish ships in the Armada of 1588 were of this description. The British relied more on heavy guns able to harass the enemy without coming into close contact. However, the Armada was defeated not so much by the big guns as by its own defects. When it was thrown into confusion by fireships off Calais, the big ships, with their large top-hamper, were not handy enough to recover their station against the winds and tides in the narrow seas.

The long-term upshot was the development of handier ships, which were armed with heavy guns mounted low down in the hull to provide stability, and which could be constructed to sail comparatively well while carrying powerful armament. These ships had a weakness, however: their sides were immensely strong and able to take great punishment, their broadsides fired on either beam were formidable, but from ahead or astern they were vulnerable. It was possible for shots hitting the bow or the stern to do great damage, much more difficult to repair than holes in the side; before its power was expended a cannonball would travel the length of the ship, wreaking more death and destruction than one passing from side to side, and it was not practicable to install much in the way of effective armament firing directly ahead or astern. A ship attacked from these directions had to take possibly crippling punishment and was not able to hit back.

The line was thus a natural formation to adopt. A ship in a line of similar ships was in a sound position – she could both give and take heavy fire on either beam, while her more vulnerable bow and stern were covered by the ships ahead and astern of her. The line of battle therefore became the standard fighting formation for more than two hundred years, and a ship of the line was the most powerful type of warship afloat.

Because of its power, the ship of the line was the principal factor in securing command of the sea. The nation which could, when necessary, bring to bear a force of line-of-battle ships sufficient to overcome anything an enemy could muster, could send its merchant ships about the world in comparative safety. A large number of smaller vessels was no answer, for since no smaller vessel could defeat a ship of the line, the nation with sufficient of them could always in the end defeat one which relied on the activities of lesser ships. If they could not be caught at sea their home ports could be blockaded, and smaller ships could not drive ships of the line away. Sea trade was not vital to the continental countries of the late eighteenth century – desirable maybe but they could get by without it; Britain could not. Sea trade was vital to Britain and consequently, in spite of many temporary failures and weaknesses, sheer necessity forced her to maintain sufficient battleships to give her the edge over potential opponents.

Britain had certain advantages in the matter of sea power. Firstly, the extent of her sea trade was so great that even the most stupid of politicians could not fail to be aware of the importance of protecting it. Secondly, the size of her merchant fleet meant that her population contained a relatively high proportion of seafarers – an obvious advantage when trying to enlarge a navy quickly. Thirdly, her geographical position was ideally suited to preventing combinations of fleets against her.

Along her south coast, Britain had ports and anchorages suitable for the largest vessels then afloat. Along the north coast of France there was nothing much between the Texel, in Holland, and Brest. Britain could therefore readily sustain a powerful fleet in the Channel, with Spithead, Plymouth, and Torbay readily accessible for temporary shelter, and from which, in most conditions, reinforcement could sail at short notice. To achieve a similar presence, France would have had to send round from Brest a fleet large enough to tackle not only any fleet the British might have at sea but, in addition, any reinforcing squadrons that might emerge at short notice from the British ports. If it suffered a defeat or ran into any kind of trouble, the prevailing westerly winds would make it difficult for a French fleet to fall back to the safety of Brest. As far as the Dutch were concerned Britain had Yarmouth, the Thames Estuary, and an anchorage in the Downs off the east coast of Kent. From those havens a constant watch on the Dutch coast could be maintained. Therefore, so long as Britain could maintain an adequate and competently led navy, a link-up between the French and Dutch navies would be almost impossible. A junction between French and Spanish fleets was not so easy to prevent but Britain was able to prevent any such combination reaching the Channel. Once an effective blockade of Brest was instituted, Britain had facilities in the south-west from which the blockading squadrons could readily be supplied. As a temporary haven in which, when conditions were such as to prevent the French putting to sea, the fleet could shelter for a short time, there was Torbay.

Command of the sea could never be absolute; on occasion the French were enabled to get to sea by errors on the part of the blockading force or by favourable combinations of circumstances. There was always the possibility of individual ships eluding the blockade; French privateers manned from the seafaring communities of Brittany and France's Atlantic coast were always a thorn in the side of British convoys. But in general the Royal Navy adequately performed its function of keeping the seas clear for Britain. That it was able to do so was attributable to the number and the efficacy of the ships of the line.

The term 'ship of the line' remained in use although, during the Napoleonic period, the custom of fighting in rigid adherence to the line of battle was becoming modified. A line of ships, controlled by flag signals, was an adequate formation in which to move a number of vessels, in a controlled manner, when not in the close presence of the enemy; but it had a number of disadvantages when battle was joined. It is clear that with the flagship somewhere near the centre of the line, the admiral's flag signals could be seen distinctly only by the ships immediately ahead and astern of him – other ships would have their line of sight at least partially obscured. Therefore passing of an instruction would have to rely on signals being repeated to frigates, which were not part of the line, or by successive repetition along the line itself. This process took appreciable time and involved delay which, in battle, was a grave handicap. Moreover, in battle there was a great deal of smoke, from the gunpowder then in use, which could effectively obscure part or all of a signal hoist.

The concept of the line as a means of mutual support contained, in itself, the risk of battles being indecisive. To avoid exposing ships' vulnerable bows to fire, the tendency was for opposing fleets to keep in lines, roughly parallel to each other, gradually drawing closer together. With fleets of any size this process could take considerable time; by the time battle was joined, there might not be much of the day left to fight in. On the open sea it was not practicable to continue action in complete darkness, the risk of confusion was too great; the action would be called off while flag signals could still be seen. Then the side which had been winning would take away ships already beaten and boarded, and damaged ships would have time to lick their wounds and make temporary repairs. In the morning, in all probability, the fleets would be well separated, the fleet which had come off worst would return to its base and its government would consider whether to refurbish it or start negotiations.

This type of battle might have served well enough in what might be called limited wars. There had been a number of these in the eighteenth century; war was declared, a trial of strength took place, and the results dictated the attitudes of the participants in the subsequent negotiations. The Napoleonic wars were not like that, however; initial revolutionary fervour and, later, Napoleon's ambitions meant that the war was not going to stop until one side or the other could not fight any more – another respect in which they resembled twentieth-century wars. A new, sterner attitude was required of commanders facing the French; the new attitude came but it took a little while.

The change in outlook may be seen both in the conduct of battles, and in the approach of the high command to the blockade. Under the command of Lord Howe and Lord Bridport in the early years of the Revolutionary war, the Channel Fleet (which was the fleet most concerned with direct defence of the country, and with the watch on the enemy's ports), was accustomed to spend most of its time in Spithead. It was considered that the ships should be preserved as much as possible from the wear and tear of seagoing; a minimum number of ships could keep an eye on the French while the bulk of the fleet polished its brasswork and was occasionally taken out for exercises in the Channel. This led to smart-looking ships and smartly executed manoeuvres; but the captains had little opportunity to develop their powers of initiative, or the subtle skills of leadership as opposed to giving orders. It was a strange anticipation of the thinking of the French, who, later in the war, consoled themselves by imagining that their ships were being preserved in harbour, while the British were wearing theirs out at sea. It was a policy which permitted the French fleet to get out to sea in May 1794 and, although technically defeated on 1 June, to ensure that a vital grain convoy got through to France. It was a policy which led to the Channel Fleet being locked into Spithead in December 1796, when it should have been off Brest. Only the mercy of Providence prevented this policy causing the loss of Ireland in 1797.

The men who, more than any others, typified the new outlook which was to permeate the navy were John Jervis (later Lord St Vincent), Adam Duncan and Horatio Nelson. Jervis was elderly and grim, Duncan was elderly and steadfast, and Nelson was young (comparatively) and ardent. Jervis was a stern apostle of duty, who recognised the value of determination unaffected by apparent odds, and hence won the battle of Cape St Vincent. He recognised the qualities of Nelson and gave him his first chance to shine. Duncan, with worn-out ships and disaffected crews, won the battle of Camperdown against the toughest opposition at sea. Nelson, though he had many faults, saw issues clearly and raised the art of leadership to the sublime. As the influence of these men (and many others who responded to their leadership) made itself felt, the navy embraced a new standard of excellence. Fleets on blockade duty stayed on station in all conditions; victory in battle was not, of itself, enough – it had to be total victory; captains learned to keep at sea, with ships maintained and crews healthy, for years instead of months. In 1800

Lord St Vincent, having taken over command of the Channel Fleet, wrote that 'seven eighths of the captains on blockade duty were only looking for an excuse to return to port'. In 1805 Nelson, when asked by Lord Barham which captains he would like for his fleet, could reply, 'Choose yourself, my Lord, the same spirit actuates the whole profession; you cannot choose wrong.'

The change exemplified by comparison of these two statements was not caused only by the attitudes of senior officers. The enlargement of the navy, and the exigencies of service in wartime, meant that many new men were being promoted and appointed to ships. As James Henderson points out in *The Frigates*, there were many more captains than there were ships to command. In peacetime, an admiral might well ask for a particular captain to be appointed to a ship under his command purely on the basis of nepotism or doing a favour to a friend. In wartime, knowing that his own reputation and possibly life might depend on the quality of his captains, he would be much more likely to ask for a man known to be good at his job. Consequently, as well as a change in the attitudes of those at the top, there was a gradual improvement in the quality of men appointed to command the battleships; the seeds of Nelson's 'band of brothers' were being sown.

Under these men the pattern of sea battles changed. The line of battle was still the normal method of approach, but once battle was joined more and more reliance was placed on the initiative and determination of each captain. It was found that the danger of taking fire from dead ahead was outweighed by the advantages of a determined attack, bringing all ships into action as quickly as possible. At the battle of Cape St Vincent, John Jervis began the action with his ships in line and under orders from the flagship; very shortly after battle was joined, prompted by an action of Nelson's, he made the signal which released his ships from the line formation and allowed freedom of action to each captain. At the Nile and at Trafalgar, the ships were launched into action with the minimum of formal order, each captain having been made thoroughly aware of what was expected of him.

The conduct of the ships of the line, when in formation, was governed by standing orders issued by the commander-in-chief of the fleet in which they were serving. Known as the *Fighting Instructions*, they were first issued by Blake in 1653 and subsequently modified by successive senior admirals as circumstances changed and, in particular, the scope of flag signals improved. They covered a great deal of ground, from the establishment of general principles of conduct to detailed instructions on maintaining position within the fleet. Lord Howe's *Instructions* of 1799 contain all relevant detailed orders. Some are fairly straightforward, such as: 'Great care is at all times to be taken not to fire at the enemy either over, or very near to, any ships of the fleet.' Others are understandable only by an expert sea- man. They make it very clear that no ship is to leave the line of battle, however hard-pressed she may be; but there is also provision for a signal giving all ships freedom to act individually, each captain decid- ing the most advantageous action for his ship. They contain such glorious English as 'If there should be found a captain so lost to all sense of honour and the great duty he owes his country, as not to exert himself to the utmost . . .'

Nelson's practice was to supplement the rigidity of the *Fighting Instructions* by personal contact with his captains, so that each one of them should know instinctively what he ought to do in any situation. Before Trafalgar, he circulated his famous Memorandum to all admirals and captains in his fleet, setting out his intentions in the coming battle and containing the words: 'In case signals can neither be seen nor perfectly understood, no captain can do very wrong if he places his ship alongside that of an enemy'.

This sentence is not only stirring in itself, but conclusively demon- strates Nelson's greatness as a commander. He does not take refuge behind the detailed plans he is spelling out; he gives each captain a simple, unequivocal order, on which he can act if in any way in doubt.

Before leaving the matter of conduct in battle, it is as well to note a couple of the rules of combat which were internationally accepted. They are somewhat chastening in that they indicate a greater degree of civilisation two hundred years ago; not an entirely fair comment, because in conditions of modern war such humanity is not practicable, but the fact remains, it does not happen now. Firstly, the convention was that a ship of the line never opened fire on a frigate unless the frigate took the first hostile action. Because of this the frigates accom- panying fleets could stand by, unharmed, while the ships of the line they were accompanying destroyed each other. This, of course, does not mean that there were not frequent and bloody battles between frigates on other duties. Secondly, and of more moment when study- ing sea battles, it was perfectly acceptable and honourable for a cap- tain, whose ship was overwhelmed and could not win, to surrender. This was done by hauling down the national flag or, if it had already been shot away, flying a white flag or the flag of his opponent. Duels between ships invariably ended with one of them having struck (that is, hauled down) her colours. It was a merciful custom, which prevented the useless slaughter of men after their ship was no longer capable of fighting.

The ships which formed the line of battle were known as first-, second- or third-rates in accordance with a system of rating introduced in the 1750s. There was nothing derogatory about the term second-rate: it was solely an indication of the number of guns carried. Ships of the size of a sloop or larger were described generally in accordance with the following system:

A first-rate carried 100 guns or more, and a second-rate 90–98 guns. First- and second-rates were known informally as three-deckers because, although they had more than three decks altogether, the main armament was carried on three decks. There were comparatively few of them, and most of them were admirals' flagships, for which they were suited because their accommodation readily provided space for an admiral and his staff.

A third-rate carried 64–84 guns. Third-rates formed the bulk of the ships of the line. The great majority of them were 74-gun ships as these were found to be the best all-round vessel for their purpose. They were handier and better sailors than first-rates, and, in terms of fire power, more economic. They were powerful enough for most purposes, and strong enough to stand fire from a first-rate, at least for a while.

Sixty-four-gun ships were obsolescent but a number were still in use in the Napoleonic wars, mainly on the North Sea station, where their reduced draught fitted them for operations in shallow waters off the Dutch coast and in the Baltic. Third-rates were informally known as two-deckers, the main armament being carried on two decks.

A fourth-rate carried 50–60 guns. They were almost obsolete, although a few were still in service. They were two-deckers, but could not be expected to slog it out with 74s.

A fifth-rate carried 32–44 guns; and a sixth-rate 20–28 on a single deck. Those with 28 or more guns were the frigates. They were smaller, faster and handier than the ships of the line. Nelson described frigates as 'the eyes of the fleet' and their function when accompanying a battle fleet was mainly that of reconnaissance vessels. They also served in convoy protection, commerce-raiding and as maids of all work. A 20-gun ship was known as a sloop of war, the smallest three-masted vessel in the navy. Its duties were similar to those of a frigate, but with limitations because of its weaker construction and fire power.

No account is taken in the ratings of the number of carronades carried. A carronade was a short, large-bore gun which fired a heavy shot a short distance. It was, therefore, effective in a yardarm-to-yardarm battle, where the enemy was only a few feet away, but not at greater ranges. A very small charge was sufficient to throw even a 24 lb ball a short distance, so the gun could be of light construction and did not need a wheeled carriage to absorb the recoil. Instead it could be mounted on a swivelling framework which, because it was light, could be carried on the upper decks of a ship. It could be aimed over a greater arc than a long gun and was deadly at close quarters. The number of carronades varied; they were carried in addition to the standard guns or, in some cases, replaced some of the lighter-calibre guns. This did not alter a ship's rating: if she had been designed as a 74-gun ship, she remained a 74-gun ship however many carronades she carried.

Among the ships of the line there were about fifteen third-rates and two second-rates for every first-rate. In each rate there were a number of classes of ship, a class being ships built to a particular design. Classes might vary slightly in dimensions and details of design but, in size, layout of decks and rig, all ships of a rate were very similar. A number were captured French ships and there was a general belief that French designs were better than British. This might well have been true in some respects, but it is necessary to be careful in making comparisons. For example, if a ship's function was to spend most of its time in port, coming out only for special occasions, it might be acceptable to sacrifice some hull space to speed and handiness. If, as was the case after the first few years of the Revolutionary war, a ship was expected to remain at sea literally for years without coming into port, the ability to carry as many stores as possible and to stand up to all weathers might well be the most important quality. It is, in any case, an unprofitable speculation; small differences in behaviour between one ship and another would, 99% of the time, be outweighed by such considerations as quality of fitting out and maintenance, and the ability and discipline of crews.

A typical 74-gun ship would have been about 165 feet long (excluding jib-boom and bowsprit), with a 46-foot beam and a draught of about 21–23 feet. A first-rate might be 20 feet longer, 5 feet wider and 3 feet deeper.

The rig was the same in every case – three masts, with square-rigged sails on each mast. Each mast was, in itself, a pretty complex structure consisting of a lower mast, a topmast and a topgallant mast.

The lower mast was a massive structure of fir, preferably spruce, perhaps 3 feet in diameter, standing on the keel of the ship and rising through the decks to a height of, say, 70 feet above the open deck. Near the top was mounted the fighting top, a platform upon which, in battle, sharpshooters would try to pick off people on an enemy deck. The whole was massively stayed by shrouds – heavy, tarred ropes stretching from beneath the top to the outside of the hull and strained tight by lanyards and deadeyes at their lower ends.

The topmast was a lighter and shorter spar lapping and fixed to the front of the mainmast. It would rise about 60 feet above the fighting top and be stayed via the edges of the fighting top to the mainmast. All its fittings were so arranged that it could, when necessary, be detached and lowered to the deck.

The topgallant mast, a similar extension to the topmast, extended to a point perhaps 155 feet above the deck, similarly fastened and braced. The topgallant mast was frequently lowered to the deck to reduce top-hamper in a storm.

The spars (known as yards) holding the sails were suspended at appropriate points on the masts, together with all the lines controlling the spars and the sails, and the blocks through which the lines passed.

The structure of each mast had to be checked, maintained and, if necessary, repaired, by the bosun and his mates so that, at the end of a year at sea, it was as capable of carrying the enormous loads imposed on it as it had been on the day the ship left port. This was long before the days of man-made fibre, wood-preservative and rust-proof alloys, and the fact that few ships came to grief through failure of rigging can only be regarded with awe as a monument to the skill and seamanship of the men responsible.

The masts, from forward to aft, were the foremast, mainmast and mizzen. The fore- and mainmasts each carried three standard square sails: in ascending order, the course, topsail and topgallant sail. During the period of the Napoleonic wars, ships of the line became equipped with an additional square sail, above the topgallant, on each mast. Known as royals, they were normally used only in light weather. The mizzen-mast was similarly rigged except that, instead of the course, it carried a large, gaff-rigged, fore-and-aft sail known as the spanker or driver.

Additional sail area could be provided on the main and foremasts by setting studdingsails (called stunsls) which were rectangular sails set either side of the topsails and topgallants on booms extended from the yards.

Almost like a fourth mast lying at about 30 degrees to the horizontal was the bowsprit, to which was attached the jib-boom. This structure carried massive stays to the foremast on which were set triangular fore-and-aft sails known as jibs. More fore-and-aft sails, known as staysails, could be set between the masts on stays running from points on one mast to higher points on the mast aft of it. In addition, two square sails, known as the spritsail and spritsail topsail could be set on yards hung below the bowsprit and jib-boom.

Setting, taking in or reefing the square sails involved men working on the yards from which the sails were suspended. The men assigned to this work, the topmen, were the most skilled seamen and, perforce, young and fit. The yards were reached by climbing the ratlines, horizontal ropes attached to the stays supporting the masts so as to form a kind of ladder. This ladder, of which the rungs were not rigid, plunged and swayed as it was being climbed, and in places sloped outwards rather than inwards so that feet had to be used to cling on with as well as to stand on. Each yard had a footrope, a horizontal line suspended about four feet below the yard; stability was achieved by standing on the footrope with heels hooked on to it, and one's elbows hooked over the yard. Incredibly, considering the sharp footholds on which they had to stand, topmen in general did not wear shoes. Their feet, in addition to becoming as tough as shoe leather, became prehensile and almost like a second pair of hands. The footropes were of hemp, even the best of which rots eventually. When it is considered that a breaking footrope, apart from the immediate loss of life, would have destroyed the morale and efficiency of the topmen for a very long time, one can only wonder again at the vigilance and skill required of those whose job it was to look after the rigging.

Within the hull the ship was divided by decks, each of which had its particular function. Below all the decks, in total darkness except when lit by dim lanterns, was the hold, which was the ship's storage area, and which was divided off into rooms or spaces allocated for particular types of stores. Those most perishable were carried near the stern, where the shape of the hull meant that the bottom was well

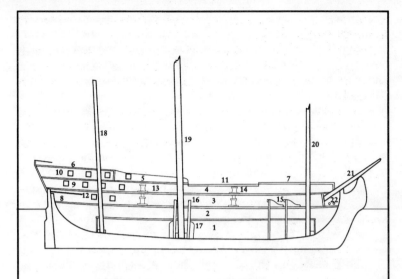

1	Hold	12	Tiller
2	Orlop deck	13	Main capstan
3	Gundeck	14	Fore capstan
4	Upper deck	15	Bitts
5	Quarterdeck	16	Pumps
6	Poop deck	17	Shot-lockers
7	Forecastle	18	Mizzen-mast
8	Gunroom	19	Mainmast
9	Wardroom	20	Foremast
10	Great cabin	21	Bowsprit
11	Undecked	22	Hawse holes

OUTLINE SECTION OF A 74-GUN SHIP

above the level amidships, and where they were least likely to be contaminated by bilge water. The spirit store was an enclosed secure area, kept locked for obvious reasons. Magazines and powder rooms were sealed-off, lead-lined compartments, having no surface in contact with the ship's sides and supported above the bottom so that the risk of water seepage was eliminated. Their entrances were protected by flash-proof curtains and lit only by lanterns separated from the interior by glass screens. The main hold area carried general stores, including food and water sealed in barrels. Fore and aft of the mainmast were the pump-wells and close to them the shot-lockers.

Above the hold was the orlop deck which was still well below the waterline. It carried the surgeon's cabin and dispensary, the cockpit, clothing store, cable tier, purser's cabin, sail room, and store rooms for the carpenter, bosun and gunner.

The hold and the orlop deck were given over to the ship's storage, servicing and maintenance. Above the orlop deck all space was devoted primarily to the ship's function as a fighting machine; the deck areas were devoted to the ship's guns or as working platforms for handling the rigging. The crew lived, in varying degrees of comfort, in such space as was left over.

In a two-decker the majority of the guns were carried on two decks – the gundeck and the upper deck. The gundeck, immediately above the orlop deck, was a little above the water-line and carried 32-pounder guns at about 11-foot intervals along each side. The aftermost gun was near the stern and the foremost at a point where the curve of the bow planking became pronounced. The after part of the deck was partitioned off to form quarters, known as the gunroom, for the midshipmen and junior warrant officers. The partitions were removed when the ship was cleared for action. The bulk of the crew slept in hammocks slung fore and aft from the beams of the deck above. They fed, seated on their seachests, from tables slung between the guns.

The upper deck was generally similar except that the guns were 18-pounders, and the after part formed the accommodation for the ship's commissioned officers, the wardroom.

Above the gundecks were the captain's quarters, the quarterdeck and the foredeck known as the forecastle. Structurally, these formed a continuous deck similar to a gundeck, with a portion in the centre unplanked, except for a walkway along either side. This left a portion of the upper deck open to the sky except for the undecked beams, above which the ships boats were normally stored. The after part of this deck formed the captain's quarters, above which was the poop deck. The captain's accommodation included a large room or great cabin about 35 feet × 20 feet, his sleeping cabin, a chart room and rooms for the use of his clerk and steward. It was luxurious in terms of space and privacy and could be furnished to any standard which the depth of the captain's pocket could provide. It was also the captain's office, conference room and area in which he could entertain when necessary. Even the captain's quarters contained their quota of guns, usually three nine-pounders on each side. When the ship was cleared for action, all domestic furnishings and all bulkheads and partitions were removed or slung out of the way from the deckhead above.

Walking forward out of his quarters, the captain would emerge on to his quarterdeck, the command centre of the ship, his duty station and that of the officer of the watch, the master, the signals midshipman, the helmsmen and others according to circumstances.

The quarterdeck extended as far as the mainmast, in front of which was the undecked area which was about 45 feet long on a third-rate. Above the opening were fixed three boat booms on which the ship's boats were carried and to which they were lashed. Usually five boats were carried, the smallest being the small cutter, about 16 feet long, and the largest the longboat, which was a substantial craft, perhaps 35 feet long with a 10-foot beam in a third-rate, and up to 50 feet long in a first-rate.

Beyond the boat booms was the forecastle deck. This might carry a number of carronades; otherwise its function was as a working platform for men controlling the jibs or foremast sails. On the outside of the hull on either side of each mast were the chains, narrow platforms strongly braced to the hull and to which the lower end of the mast stay tackles were attached. Their effect was to improve the efficiency of the stays by spreading their anchorage further from the foot of the mast than the edge of the deck. The foremast chains also formed a platform from which the lead line was used when sounding for depth.

The poop deck formed the roof of the captain's quarters and was a working platform for controlling the sheets, braces and halliards of the mizzen-mast.

The wood used in the construction of the ship was oak, ideally English oak. This wood was preferred to any other because of its strength and lasting qualities. Some smaller ships were built in India of teak which, in nearly every respect, is the perfect ship- or boat-building timber, being strong, hard and almost totally resistant to rot. It had, however, one fatal disadvantage as a material for warships: a large proportion of the casualties in battle was caused not by direct hits but by flying splinters, and wounds made by teak splinters invariably turned septic. Those made by oak splinters did not. In the days before antiseptics this was a major consideration.

It took 80 acres of oak trees to make one 74-gun ship and by the end of the wars, the problem of timber supply was becoming critical. Supplies held out just long enough, however, and later in the century steel took over before oak gave out altogether.

The form of construction was massive. Throughout the major part of the hull, where the guns were carried, planking 4 inches thick, increasing to $8\frac{1}{2}$ inches in the vicinity of the gundeck, was laid on frames about 12 to 15 inches square which were virtually touching from stem to stern. Inside the frames was a second layer of planking with a minimum thickness of 4 inches, and inside this layer were more frames, something like 14 inches by 24, at about 8-foot centres. Thus, over most of the hull, there was a total thickness of about 20 inches of solid wood, which increased to over 2 feet in places, not counting internal framing. The deck beams were joined to the frames with large brackets or knees; between adjacent decks, and between the orlop beams and the keel, were sturdy pillars. The whole formed a sort of gigantic wooden box with very thick sides and extensive internal bracing, immensely strong.

The great enemy of wooden ships was rot. Very little was known of the different kinds of wood rot and their causes, and there were no effective wood-preservatives. The necessarily solid nature of warship construction involved the building in of unventilated cavities, which were breeding grounds for rot, and, since ships were mostly built out of doors freshwater dampness was inevitably present from the very beginning. Only constant vigilance by ships' carpenters and frequent extensive overhauls in dry dock kept the fleets in fighting condition.

Masts were of fir, which with hemp and flax came principally from the Baltic states, a fact which had considerable influence on Britain's policies throughout the wars, and which led directly to one sea battle. Indeed, the importance of Britain's trade with the Baltic played its part in Napoleon's fatal decision to invade Russia.

All the massive strength and complexity of a finished ship was achieved entirely by hand tools, with only the crudest of lifting devices, and a 74-gun ship could be completed in well under two years. A very high proportion of the labour force involved was highly skilled, and the speed of building suggests not only a high degree of organising ability in yard managers but a great deal of mutual co-operation between the tradesmen involved. Insofar as this was typical of substantial enterprises of the time, it may offer some clue to the character of the people. A man whose livelihood is in his own skill is likely to be a more contented and well-balanced individual than one whose job is pressing buttons – whether on a machine or a computer. Perhaps that is why people, both in and out of the services, could stand up to hardships that seem to us unendurable – they were less neurotic.

The ingenuity and fitness for purpose achieved by the builders did not stop with the fabric of the ship. Much of its equipment was equally impressive, in its use of existing technology to produce a neat and workmanlike solution to a problem; for example, the pumps, which in a wooden warship were as vital to its continued existence as the masts and sails – in some circumstances more so. Even in a victorious battle, a ship could be badly damaged on or below the waterline and her victory would be a hollow one if she sank as a result of it. Holes below the waterline could seldom be temporarily plugged, as they could higher up in the hull; often the only action that could be taken was to fother the hole. This consisted of man-oeuvring over the hole, from outside the hull, a mat made out of canvas and rope yarn, with ropes fastened to each corner. Once over the hole, the pressure of water kept the mat in place, and the flow into the hull would be greatly restricted, but seldom stopped entirely. The ship would then depend totally on her pumps until she could get to a port with suitable facilities or until she could be beached.

The pumps were masterpieces in their simplicity and fitness for their purpose. There were four of them, grouped round the mainmast on the gundeck, picking up water from the lowest point of the hull. Each consisted of a chain, not unlike a greatly enlarged bicycle chain, with discs attached to it like collars at regular intervals. The chain passed over a large wheel turned by cranked handles on the gundeck, down a loose-fitting timber tube to the bilge, round a roller and up through a tube inside which the discs fitted closely. At the bottom of its travel, on entering the rising tube each disc took with it a slug of water which, on reaching the gundeck, was discharged into a cistern

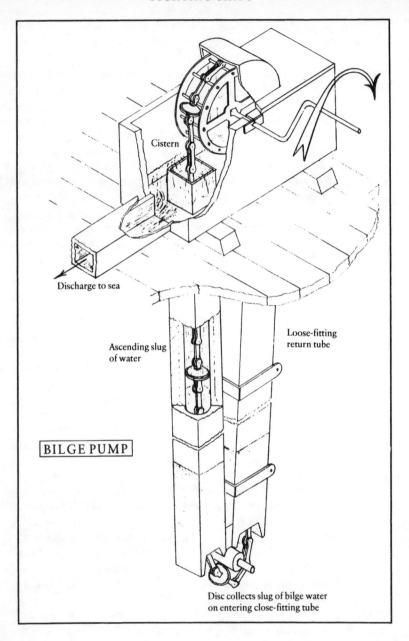

Cistern

Discharge to sea

Ascending slug
of water

Loose-fitting
return tube

BILGE PUMP

Disc collects slug of bilge water
on entering close-fitting tube

and thence overside. It was hard work to operate but it was efficient and simple, and very little could go wrong with it. If one were damaged during an action, the ship's carpenter and his mates could quickly repair it. The capacity of four pumps was similar to that of a water main supplying a town of 30,000 people. So long as the intake of water could be kept below this rate, successive shifts of men at the pump handles could keep the ship afloat.

A ship of the line carried six anchors, two bower anchors, normally carried in a position on either bow from which they could readily be let go, two sheet anchors (in effect spare bowers), and two smaller anchors, used when moving the ship short distances in harbour. The main anchor cables were of hemp and 600 feet long, 7-inch diameter in the case of third-rates, and $9\frac{1}{2}$ inches in first-rates. To control cables of this sort of size, which would require a man every few feet to move them at all, was a major problem. They were too big to be used on any capstan and could not readily be wrapped round any form of cleat or bitts. The solution was the use of messengers and stoppers, lengths of rope of more manageable size which could be attached to the anchor cable to control it.

Each ship had two capstans which are a form of winch with the drum vertical instead of horizontal. Each capstan had two drums complete with drumheads (into which the capstan bars were inserted); one drum was on the gundeck and one on the upper deck, and they worked on a common vertical shaft or spindle which ran through both decks. A capstan could be used by men on the gundeck, or the upper deck, or both. It could be used for many purposes, whenever a strong pull was required on a line which could be led to one of the capstan drums by blocks appropriately sited. When it was used to control an anchor cable, a messenger or stopper was employed.

A messenger was a length of rope, of a size which could be used on a capstan, joined end to end to form a continuous ring about 200 feet in circumference. It was wound several times round the capstan and led over appropriate guides and through blocks so that a length of it lay along the route of the anchor cable from its hawse hole to the cable tier amidships. The messenger was then nipped (fastened) to the anchor cable near the hawse hole, and, by heaving the messenger round the capstan, the cable was hauled aboard; when the fastening nipping the messenger to the cable approached the capstan, it was cast off, a second fastening having already been applied near the hawse hole. By this means, the messenger brought the cable steadily

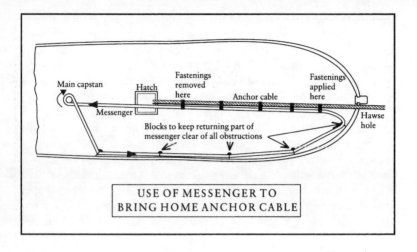

Main capstan Hatch Fastenings removed here Anchor cable Fastenings applied here

Messenger

Blocks to keep returning part of messenger clear of all obstructions

Hawse hole

USE OF MESSENGER TO BRING HOME ANCHOR CABLE

aboard. In practice, a series of fastenings was applied in rotation, put on near the hawse hole and taken off as the capstan was approached; by tradition boys among the crew were employed on this duty, hence the term 'nipper' for a boy, especially one of a dextrous and lively nature. A stopper was a length of smaller-diameter rope, one end of which could be fastened to the cable using a hitch which would not slide. By hauling on the other end, using a tackle or a capstan, the strain of the anchor cable could be taken on the stopper.

The ship had two sets of bitts located on the lowest gundeck, near the bow, one set aft of the other. Bitts were heavy timber frames, strongly built into the structure of the ship, to which the inboard end of the anchor cable was attached. The anchor cable could be temporarily lashed to the bitts by smaller-diameter rope, or held more permanently by wrapping the cable about the bitts as a small-diameter line is wrapped round a cleat or a belaying pin. To manhandle the cable round the bitts, or to remove it after use was a heavy task for a gang of men which could only be done when there was no strain on the rope being handled; this was the reason for two sets of bitts. When raising the anchor, the cable was first lashed to the foremost bitts; then, with the lashing temporarily taking the strain, the cable

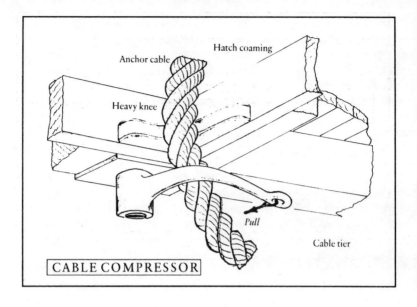

CABLE COMPRESSOR

was unhitched from the aftermost bitts and laid out alongside the messenger. Once the messenger was taking the strain, the lashing could be removed.

When letting go the anchor, the cable running out was checked with a simple friction brake called a compressor. This was a heavy iron lever arranged so that a pull on the end of it squeezed the cable against a knee or rubbing pad in the corner of the hatchway above the cable tier. With a sufficiently powerful tackle on the lever, the progress of the cable could be gradually slowed down and stopped when sufficient length of anchor cable was out. The cable was then lashed to the foremost bitts and the compressor released; finally the cable was manhandled on to the aftermost bitts and the lashing removed.

The source of power for dealing with the huge loads represented by anchors and their cables was men in large numbers. In a fully manned ship large numbers of men were available – many times the crew of the largest merchant ship. However, there were many duties and few of the crew were specialists; almost any one of them had to be able to handle sails, work guns or form part of a team controlling heavy loads. None of these duties was more exacting than handling the heavy, intractable anchor cable. To move it about the deck, or over the bitts, required many men, working shoulder to shoulder in perfect unison: a false move by any one man could cause all kinds of chaos. When heaving on the compressor-tackle, too much force could cause destructive snatching loads on cable and ship; too little could allow the cable to get out of hand. Orders had to be both delicate and unmistakable, and they had to be carried out with precision by every man involved. The work might have to be done on a heaving deck or – as at the Nile and at Copenhagen – in the midst of battle. Yet again, there can only be awe for the skills of the crews.

All the craftsmanship in the construction of the ship and all the skills of the crew had one purpose, to bring into action, at any required time and place, the reason for the ships' existence – their guns. Apart from carronades, these were much the same as they had been in Drake's time, cast-iron barrels mounted on heavy timber carriages firing solid cast-iron shot. There were three standard sizes described by the weight of shot fired: 32 lb, 18 lb, and 9 lb. On ships of the line 32-pounders were employed on the lowest gundeck, 18-pounders on the upper deck (or two highest gundecks in the case of a first-rate) and 9-pounders on the quarterdeck. Late in the Napoleonic period, a number of 9-pounders were replaced with 12-pounders.   Each gun had fourteen controlling devices or tools associated with it, most of which had to be operated every time it fired.

1. A gunport-tackle to hold open the gunport.
2. A train-tackle to hold the gun back, clear of the ship's side, while it was being loaded.
3. A rammer to ram down the barrel, in succession, the cartridge, the ball and the wad.
4. A section of quill filled with gunpowder, to be inserted into the touch-hole to carry the firing spark to the cartridge.
5. A handspike with which to heave round the back of the carriage to adjust the gun's direction of fire.
6. The quoin, a wedge to be pushed under the breech end of the barrel to adjust the elevation.
7. and 8. Gun-tackles, one on each side, with which to haul the gun into its firing position after loading.
9. A flintlock firing mechanism, operated by a cord enabling the gun captain to keep out of the way of the recoil while firing the gun.

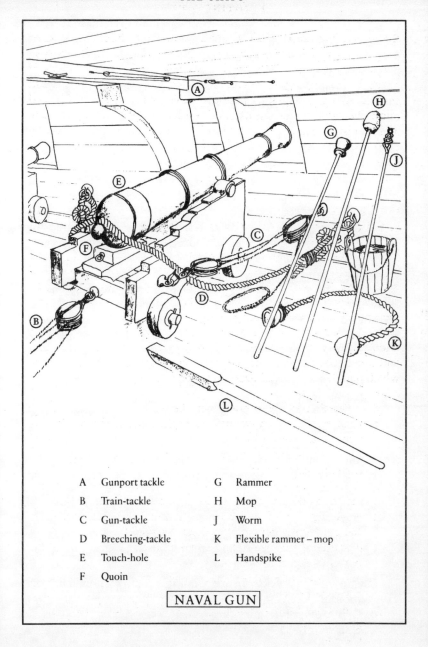

A	Gunport tackle	G	Rammer
B	Train-tackle	H	Mop
C	Gun-tackle	J	Worm
D	Breeching-tackle	K	Flexible rammer – mop
E	Touch-hole	L	Handspike
F	Quoin		

NAVAL GUN

10. A slow match kept glowing for use should the flintlock fail.
11. A breeching-tackle, a heavy rope threaded through a ring on the breech and fastened to the ship's side on either side of the gun, to limit its recoil.
12. A sponge or mop on a long handle, to damp out any glowing particles left in the barrel before reloading.
13. A length of thick rope with a rammer at one end and a sponge at the other. This was for use in close engagement with the hull touching that of the enemy; in these conditions the long wooden handle could not be passed out of the gunport in order that the inner end could enter the mouth of the gun, but the flexible rope could be worked in. It obviously took more time and was a last resort.
14. A worm, like a large corkscrew on a long handle, used for extracting the wad and cartridge, should it be necessary to unload the gun.

There were no printed orders for gun drill until after the end of the wars. Instead there was a standard sequence of commands and operations, which varied in detail from ship to ship in accordance with the foibles of each captain. Any gun drill, however, had perforce to include the following operations:

1. Gun held back with train-tackle,
2. Barrel swabbed out,
3. Cartridge (made up in paper container) passed from behind gun and rammed home,
4. Ball taken from ready-use rack or passed from behind gun and rammed home,
5. Wad – a ball of rags – rammed home to prevent ball rolling out,
6. Gun hauled up to firing position using gun-tackles,
7. Running ends of gun-tackles carefully placed so that they cannot tangle with carriage as gun recoils,
8. Gun captain inserts powder-filled quill into touch-hole, piercing cartridge,
9. Gun captain checks aim and elevation (a purely nominal operation in close combat),
10. Gun captain fires gun,
11. Gun recoils,

12. Gun held with train-tackle and gun captain stops vent to reduce wear from corrosive gases.

Process repeated.

A 32-pounder weighed about 3 tons, and the guns were spaced at about 11-foot centres. As the carriage and its wheels were about five feet wide, there was about six feet of space between adjacent guns. This was the space in which most of these operations had to be carried out by some members of both gun teams. Allowing a few inches' margin, each man had a strip about two feet wide to work in: he had to heave on tackles, pass cartridges and shot, stand clear of the recoil, all within this strip. Step back six inches too far and he might collide with a man working on the next gun; step forward six inches too far and he could lose his toes. Once established, the drill would have to be as perfect and as synchronised as that of a dance troupe, each man treading on the same few square inches of deck every time. All this in thick smoke and continuous noise, and possibly while stupid with fatigue – close action could last for three hours or more. Mercifully, once into the swing of it, a man would become an automaton; without time to think much about his tiny, noisy, smoke-filled world suddenly ending in an explosion of splinters.

The best crews could fire a shot every sixty seconds; it could easily take a less well-trained crew twice as long: thus a well-trained ship meeting a similar vessel with an inexperienced crew could, for all practical purposes, be twice as powerful as her opponent. It is easy to see why a French ship at sea after months in harbour faced great odds against a British ship six months at sea with gunnery drill every day.

The shape of a frigate or smaller vessel was designed for optimum sailing performance and the cost of making the hull the best shape and also big enough to accommodate the required guns, men and stores was acceptable. Consequently, frigates could sail as well as any square-rigged ship of the period. The design of a 74-gun ship contained an element of compromise, and this element was even greater in the case of a first-rate. A ship of the line was designed primarily to be powerful; its sailing qualities were important, but not more so than its ability to carry guns; it could have been designed to sail better, but this would have been at the expense of something else – guns and stores carried, or economy. Over a long period the design of the ships evolved as the best all-round compromise between power, sailing qualities and expense. Consequently, the ship of the line was well suited to its purpose, but with certain limitations, perhaps the most apparent of which was its inability to sail close to the wind.

A ship of the line could readily sail in any direction away from the wind. If the wind were from the south she could sail east, north, west or any direction in between with ease. To make headway in any direction south of east or west was a different matter. Close-hauled (that is, with her sails set as close to a fore-and-aft direction as practicable) she could point her bow ESE or WSW; however, because her hull was rather slab-sided, the wind would, at the same time, be blowing her *sideways* so that the actual direction achieved would be more like East by South or West by South. This handicap was not quite so disastrous as might be thought. In the first place, even though the wind in a particular area may blow mostly from a particular direction, it does not, in most areas, do so *all* the time; therefore it was usually worth waiting for the wind to change to a more favourable direction. Secondly, the effect on the enemy was probably the same – if you could not sail in a particular direction, neither could your enemy. Thirdly, prevailing winds in different parts of the world are in different directions. For example, if you could not sail direct to America, you might well be able to get there by going south to the Canary Isles and, there, picking up the north-east trade winds which, almost continuously, blow east to west.

Nevertheless, there were occasions when ships had to make progress in a direction opposite to that of the wind. For example, consider the case of a ship at St Helen's, Spithead, wishing to sail down the Channel to Torbay, the wind being due south. Once clear out into the Channel, a south wind would be fair for Torbay, but from leaving Spithead until clear of the Isle of Wight it would be dead against her desired course. A north wind would serve her purpose ideally, but if it were too far to the north-east she could not get out of Spithead, and, if too far to the north-west, it would be foul once she cleared the island. So, rather than wait, perhaps many days, for the perfect wind, the ship would leave, and until clear of the island she would beat to windward, that is sail as close to the desired direction as she could, which would initially be East by South. This would be fine until she began to approach the rocks and shallows off Selsey Bill, when she would have to change to the alternative best southerly direction she could manage, West by South. Once again, all would

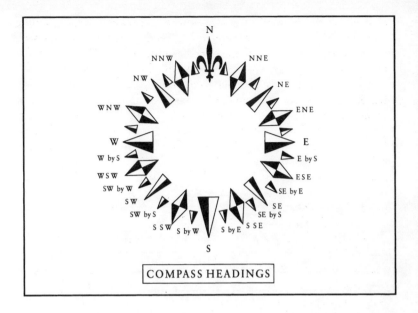

COMPASS HEADINGS

be well until she found herself approaching the eastern shore of the Isle of Wight when she would have to change direction to East by South once more. This time, with luck, East by South would take her clear of the dangers off Selsey Bill and soon thereafter she could change direction again. A course of West by South would now take her clear of the Isle of Wight and out into the Channel and she would soon be able to turn west for Torbay. (This example somewhat oversimplifies the shallows outside Spithead and ignores the matter of tides which would, of course, be used to the best advantage.)

At each change of direction, the captain of the ship could do one of two things; he could cause the ship to 'wear' or to 'tack'. To wear is to change direction by turning the bows of the ship away from the wind, and continue turning so that the bows pass through a direction pointing straight downwind and finally settle pointing in the desired new direction. In our example the bows would turn to larboard from East by South to the north-east through north, north-west and finally end up pointing West by South. From a ship-handling point of view, this is a comparatively easy operation; adjustment of the sails is necessary, but the precise moment of adjusting them is not critical, and provided no one does something absolutely stupid, the ship will

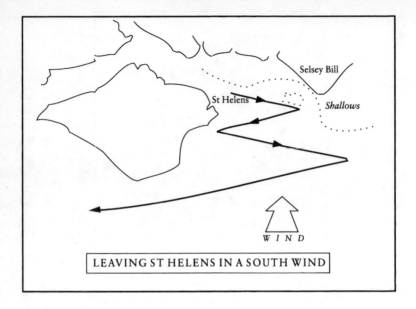

St Helens

Selsey Bill

Shallows

W I N D

LEAVING ST HELENS IN A SOUTH WIND

turn and eventually end up on the desired new course. However, the operation takes time, and for most of that time the ship is being taken in the opposite direction to that in which the captain wishes to go. In our example, by the time the ship had changed from pointing East by South to West by South, she could easily have been half a mile further north (that is, downwind) than she was when she started the turn, which might have been disastrous, the ship could have ended up on the mud off Selsey Bill. Even if this did not happen, a lot of ground would have been lost. So our captain would not wear, he would tack.

To tack is to change direction by turning the ship towards the direction from which the wind is coming, so that the bows at one moment point dead to windward, and then continue turning until they settle on the new course. If it is skilfully done, very little ground is lost in the process. In the example quoted, if the captain controlled the tacking operation correctly at each change of direction, the ship would be in no danger of drifting far downwind, and he would have very little lost ground to make up. The snag is that to tack a ship – especially a square-rigged ship – correctly, the co-ordination of rudder and sail-handling has to be exact. The process involves hauling the

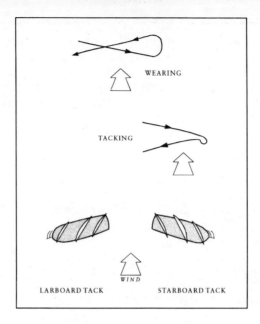

WEARING

TACKING

LARBOARD TACK   STARBOARD TACK

WIND

sails on the mainmast round from one side of the mast to the other at precisely the right moment, a job requiring proper control of the efforts of many hands. If the operation is not done properly, the ship will not go round; she may fall back on the original course or she may hang 'in irons', that is, pointing dead to windward, being blown astern and not swinging round in one direction or the other. There are ways of recovering from this situation but they all take time during which the ship will drift downwind and towards any dangers there may be astern. Thus, tacking was a highly skilled operation and in many cases wearing would be considered a lubberly alternative. Nevertheless, when there is sea room, there are occasions when wearing has advantages. At the battle of Cape St Vincent, Nelson did not tack out of the line, but ordered Captain Miller to wear. He knew it could be done at once, without taking men from the guns, and the comparatively simple sail-handling could be done by the men already stationed on deck.

An example of an occasion when a captain had no choice but to tack, and to get it right first time, is that of a ship which was embayed. It could happen, especially on blockade duty, that a ship found itself, possibly as a result of a sudden wind change, close inshore, in a bay, with an onshore wind. At each end of the bay there might be headlands stretching out to sea right in the path of the ship's route out to open sea. In this situation the ship would beat to windward and change direction at each end of the bay. Unless the bay were large, with deep water close inshore, there would be no question of the ship wearing, since in doing so she would lose more ground than could be made good by the time she came to the opposite headland. The captain would have to tack his ship close inshore, and get it right *every time*. This was a common occurrence among ships on blockade duty, and some, indeed, were caught and succumbed; almost all, however, came out of it time and again and once more one must admire the seamanship of the captains and their crews.

Quite apart from its use in connection with changing course, the word 'tack' will be encountered referring to the ship's situation relative to the wind direction. When a ship is sailing steadily along and the wind is reaching the sails by coming over the right-hand side of the ship facing forward, or the starboard side, she is said to be on the starboard tack. When the wind is coming over the other side, she is said to be on the port tack or, in the days of Nelson, on the larboard tack. If the wind is coming from dead aft or nearly so, the ship is said to be running.

CHAPTER 3

Crews

The officers of the navy were professionals; none of them joined 'for the duration', and no one joined because it gave any social cachet. Most of them were middle-class (it was not a profession for aristocrats), and most were dedicated men; it was too hard a life for dilettantes.

To anyone intending to become a naval officer, it was a great help to know someone in senior naval circles. Unlike the army, in which commissions could be purchased, the only way to a naval commission was six years' service at sea, at the end of which time the examinations for lieutenant could be taken. Usually, these six years were spent as a midshipman. There were channels by which a boy without influence could become a midshipman but they were few; by far the most usual method was to have a relative or family friend who was a captain or admiral and get taken into his ship, if not as a midshipman then as a captain's servant, which, in the end, amounted to much the same thing. The young aspirant was thus thrown in at the deep end of shipboard life and, with a minimum of formal tuition, had to absorb the intricacies of operating a ship of war.

It was brutal but effective; most boys managed to adapt themselves and their conduct as necessary. The fate of a boy, once joined, who found himself a fish out of water hardly bears thinking about, and it is to be hoped that he could get out as soon as possible. There were a number of fiddles, more or less winked at, by which nepotism could ease the path – records could be falsified to provide six years' service before the elapse of six years, and ages could be exaggerated – but everyone had to pass the examination for lieutenant. This was conducted by a board of three officers and although favouritism could creep in, it was unlikely to be a very great influence. It is not easy to deceive in a verbal examination and there is always one natural check on nepotism – there is little credit to be gained by pushing a protégé who is incompetent.

Virtually all officers, therefore, started their commissioned careers with a degree of competence. There were no special branches and every naval officer had, perforce, to know how to sail a ship. Once started, whom one knew and luck played a great part; not very surprising since this has always been the case and is likely to remain so. What was a little different was the shamelessness, or perhaps one could say the lack of hypocrisy, with which influence was looked for and applied. It was considered perfectly normal for someone with connections to use them, and for people with power to use it in favour of their friends. It may not have been just but who expected justice?

There was great incentive for an officer to use every available means for self-advancement because it was important to get to the rank of captain at an early age if at all possible. Once a captain, promotion through the various grades of admiral was purely by seniority; therefore the younger you could become a captain, the greater your chances of becoming an admiral of the fleet. It sounds a crazy system but there were checks and balances. There were a great many captains and admirals on half-pay without an appointment; being promoted to a rank was not at all the same as being employed in that rank. Consequently someone promoted, by influence, beyond his capacity would simply find himself not employed. Conversely, if it was desired to promote to admiral a bright captain, it could be done – those captains senior to him (and presumably not so bright) would be promoted and then put on half-pay. It must be remembered that this was a different age and there were many customs which seem strange now. Army commissions had to be purchased – arising from a perfectly logical desire to prevent footloose adventurers from getting to high rank and then using their position and their troops to contrive *coups d'état*; in the Spanish Navy and in the old Royalist French forces, each officer had to have a certificate of nobility. In the French revolutionary navy, officers were made on a different but equally unsatisfactory basis. Certainly the Royal Navy system, though it produced some demonstrably bad officers, produced a high proportion of very good ones. Even the unfairness sometimes produced good results: Nelson, by having an uncle who was a senior official in the hierarchy, became a post captain at the age of 20. (Any officer in command of a vessel was known by the courtesy title of captain; a post captain was a captain by rank and would remain a captain whether appointed to a ship or not.) Because he thus became a captain at a much earlier age than might be expected under any strictly impartial system, he became an admiral in the vigour of early middle age, so that the country had the benefit of his genius in its full flower.

A 74-gun ship normally carried the captain and four lieutenants. A first-rate carried two additional lieutenants; as a flagship (her normal function), she would also have the admiral and his staff. There would also be the Marine officers, two or three on a 74, more on a first-rate, according to the duty on hand. Below the commissioned ranks but of high standing and importance were the warrant officers; the master and his mates were responsible under the captain for navigation, the boatswain, carpenter and gunner kept the fabric of the vessel and its equipment in good condition. These men were long-serving volunteers, masters of their craft and, so far as any members of a team can be singled out, essential to the ship's well-being. Lower in rank but also performing key functions were the many senior petty officers, such as the sailmaker, boatswain's mates and quartermasters. They too were normally men who had volunteered for the navy and of long service. Midshipmen were officers in training; they received instruction in navigation and other nautical skills from the master and other warrant officers, and performed duties comparable to those of petty officers as they acquired experience.

The Marines were all volunteers, although, as in the army, a number of men volunteered from some form or other of necessity, and some were enticed into enlisting by plausible recruiting sergeants. Finally there were the seamen, among whom may be included junior petty officers and specialists. Some were genuine volunteers – adventurous souls who liked the life, or perhaps found life in the navy a refuge from troubles ashore. Many were pressed men, mostly merchant seamen swept up by the press gangs. The manner in which pressing was carried out – without warning – must have caused hardship for many individuals; but, in general, the press was an occupational hazard for merchant seamen, and the majority probably accepted their fate with philosophy, as conscripts do in the present century. Then there were the quota men, victims of a system in which the authorities of counties or major towns were required to produce a quota of men for the navy. Many were men in some form of trouble, criminals offered release from jail or small debtors offered immunity from legal processes if they would join the navy. All had joined as a result of some form of coercion or inducement. They were looked down on by the others as they were neither seamen nor true volunteers. It is, however, probably unfair to think of them as necessarily jailbirds and hardened criminals, for justice was hard in those days and many a man was jailed for what today would be considered a minor matter.

There was one thread of hope running through the life of a seaman: prize money. Captured vessels were paid for by the government and the proceeds distributed to the crews responsible. True, the apportioning of the money between different ranks was grossly inequitable; a lucky captain could become rich for the rest of his life, a very lucky seaman might, if he were financially sophisticated, set himself up in a shop or a small public house. Nevertheless, it had the eternal fascination of fortuitous money, and a man of optimistic nature could always hope.

The total number of men carried by a 74-gun ship was about 600, on a first-rate possibly 800. Numbers varied very considerably according to circumstances and the time a ship had been away from her home port. Inevitably, when considering the manning of the navy in the Napoleonic wars, there arises the spectre of brutal discipline and intolerable hardship; phrases like 'rum, sodomy and the lash' and 'Flog the man, Mr Christian' come readily to mind, as does the fact that the navy mutinied in 1797. The present-day Royal Navy places considerable emphasis on the 'cat o' nine tails' when escorting visitors round HMS *Victory*; perhaps because it is easier to attract interest like this than by attempting to explain to laymen the fascinating intricacies of the ship. Or perhaps because it is pleasing to contemplate the contrast between such dark matters and the agreeable and well set up young men, clearly members of an efficient and enlightened service, who show us round.

It would be nice to think that, in spite of the mutinies which took place, the victories and successful operations of the time were achieved by brave men more or less willingly doing their duty, rather than by cowed unfortunates driven by fear of cruel punishment. What is the truth?

By modern standards life in the navy was hard; but it has to be considered in relation to civilian life at the time, which was also hard. If the discipline of the navy was harsh, so too was the discipline of civil law. Hanging was the punishment for a great many offences which would hardly merit a suspended sentence today. Kind and good people lived, without being unduly oppressed, in a society which tolerated bare-fist prize fighting, bull-baiting, bear-baiting and cock-fighting. So, before being too sure of the feelings of a sailor on a ship of the line, thinking has to be adjusted to the standards of that time; which is not easy to do. It is difficult enough for a civilian to form an accurate concept of service life in his own time. It is, however, possible to form a judgement based on well-established facts, and facts which are timeless, rather than on impressions.

Modern historians such as J. A. M. Rodger and J. D. Byrns Jr have shown that naval discipline was not, in fact, less merciful than civil law at the time and that, in courts martial, the navy was in some ways in advance of conventional thinking. Even a hasty look at the court martial records indicates that they were by no means unfeeling instruments of a system. When the Articles of War (the navy's penal code) allowed only death as the sentence, it was frequently passed with a recommendation to mercy, and reasons were often found for reducing a serious charge. It is improbable, therefore, that official justice was a major cause of discontent.

Nor should hardship be confused with unhappiness. Provided that life is sustainable, hardship, as such, has little to do with happiness. It is what caused the hardship that counts. Thus a mountaineer, of his own volition halfway up Everest, in a tiny tent, hungry and tired, but with faith in his companions, may be happy; a warm and well-fed sailor, deprived of a cup of tea because of his officer's inability to organise, may be resentful and miserable.

It is necessary, therefore, to look beyond the exacting nature of naval discipline and the obvious hardships of life on board in order to find the source of men's happiness or otherwise, and what caused them to mutiny. There are at least two other factors which affect a serviceman's outlook.

The most immediate factor is the everyday attitude of his officers, as it affects every detail of his life. A quotation from the letters of Private Wheeler, a soldier in the Peninsular war, says it all: writing of possible future service under the Duke of Wellington he says, '. . . we should always be as well supplied with rations *as the nature of the service would admit* . . . what can a soldier desire more?' Note the words in italics; he does not ask for the moon, he asks only that his officers shall do the best they can in the prevailing conditions. If an officer tries to be just, and to look after the well-being of his men, the average serviceman will respond. If not, not.

The second factor is the conditions of service laid down by government regulations. These were, for the most part, outside the province of ships' officers and they greatly affected the sailor's long-term welfare.

With regard to the effect of officers, there was only one officer on a ship who really mattered, the captain. The captain was the fountainhead; everything depended on him. If he were a good commander all subordinate officers, commissioned, warrant and petty, would work in accordance with his wishes and methods. Life on board would be good; it might be uncomfortable or boring or terrifying, but it would not be soul-destroying. Injustices and unnecessary annoyances would, as far as humanly possible, be eliminated. Such a captain would inspire respect, and a man working under someone he respects is halfway to being happy on that account alone. If the captain were not a good commander there would be a great difference. If he were well-intentioned, things might still be not too bad if the subordinate officers were good men; but if he were an evil man, or a weak man with evil subordinates, then indeed the ship could become a hell on earth. Here was a big difference between the navy and the army, or between the navy then and the navy in modern times. In the army a unit commander would, a lot of the time, be under the eye of his general, and his officers and men would be in touch with other people outside the unit. Any significant peculiarities in his conduct would leak out. Similarly, a modern ship's captain, thanks to modern communications, is no longer completely isolated. But in Napoleonic times a ship's captain was, for long periods, supreme. There was no one to vet his conduct and there was no appeal against his actions. Consequently, if a captain were a bad lot he could make life literally unbearable. On occasion this happened and there were isolated mutinies as a result. Fortunately, such things were rare, and usually as a result of mental imbalance. A captain's future career, and perhaps his life, might depend on the conduct of his crew in a crisis. No sane man would wreck his chances by destroying his crew's morale and neglecting to look to their health. Cowed, ill-nourished men do not win battles. That serious ill treatment by officers was comparatively rare was indicated in the 1797 mutinies; as will be seen, such matters were not among the major grievances.

In the case of conditions of service as laid down by regulations, one is chiefly concerned with rations, leave and pay.

The official daily ration was ample in bulk. In theory, it totalled about 3 lbs of food per day, including biscuit, meat, dried peas, oatmeal, butter and cheese. The problems were peculation on the part of suppliers and pursers and lack of means to preserve food in palatable condition. Meat came pickled in brine in barrels, and it was all too easy for a contractor to include more than a fair proportion of gristle and bone and to give short weight; by the time the barrel was opened, the ship might be thousands of miles away. Biscuit was a form of bread that would keep (it was rock-hard and infested with weevils), butter went rancid and cheese became hard and stale. All the same, it was a better diet than a good many people lived on. A lot depended on the captain; an energetic captain would do battle with food contractors whenever he could, make sure that the cooking facilities were organised as well as might be, and look for opportunities to provide variety from local sources whenever possible.

Leave was rare and uncertain. For fear of desertion, it was commonly the practice to allow no shore leave in home or other civilised ports. Instead, when a ship was in port for any length of time 'wives' were allowed on board. The only space on board for the entertainment of women was the open deck on which the crew lived and some of the women were, in fact, wives. The feelings of a young, newly married couple whose only contact with each other had to be in such circumstances are perhaps best left unimagined. Yet this system did not cause the public outrage which it would today, perhaps because the reason behind it was not perversity on the part of the authorities, but what was seen as pragmatic necessity. Communications of the time did not permit of a properly considered and well-regulated system of conscription (although Napoleon, with a despotic bureaucracy managed it). A man enlisted by the rough-and-ready methods of the press might be philosophical about it but did not feel any sense of public obligation, as he might have done if conscripted under a system in which all men were liable. In consequence desertion was not felt to be shameful. There was no police force and virtually no means of recovering a deserter once away from the port; with the navy overstretched and short of men, even a small number of crew missing could seriously affect the efficient running of a ship.

So the authorities might be said to have some sort of a case. To a man not intending to desert and in sight of his home port, the refusal of leave must have been bitter and frustrating but his situation was not, in essentials, unlike that of many others; soldiers, once overseas, got no leave until the campaign was over – in Spain this could be five years and certainly was so for the Duke of Wellington, who did not leave the Continent for the whole of that time. Collingwood, as C-in-C Mediterranean, did not leave his flagship for a similar period. Even with the fantastically improved communications of the twentieth century, in World War II many men did not see their families for four years. So the absence of leave, though a cause of sadness, was not a major cause of exasperation.

Pay was unjust by any standards. Not only had it not changed since the days of Charles II, in spite of greatly increased prices, but it was not paid in cash. Men were paid in promissory notes which could only be exchanged for cash at their ship's port of commission. A ship might not return to its port of commission for years. As no one can live on promissory notes, seamen had to sell them to land-sharks for a fraction of their proper value. It is hard to understand how such a perverse system could have survived as long as it did, and how those admirals and captains who were men of principle – and many were – could have let it go on without protest. The probable answer is that it is not easy even for senior officers to make too strong a protest to their superiors, and that the government, harassed by lack of money, did not wish to know.

In 1797, the Channel Fleet, responsible for the blockade of Brest, was still based at Spithead under the nominal command of Lord Howe. Lord Howe was a good man but elderly and in poor health; it was not possible for him to display the vigour required, both to keep the fleet sternly to its duties, and to maintain morale within it in the face of a dull and uninspiring routine. The effective commander was Alexander Hood, Lord Bridport, a member of the famous Hood family and a worthy man, but not the great man the situation desperately needed. The time when the whole fleet would remain almost constantly at sea had yet to come. The man who was to achieve this, Lord St Vincent, was still C-in-C of the Mediterranean Fleet, and it is a measure of the decadence that had set in that his methods were viewed with alarm and distaste by the officers of the Channel fleet. There is a story that, at dinner with an admiral present, a captain of the Channel Fleet proposed, unrebuked, the toast, 'May the discipline of the Mediterranean Fleet never be introduced into the Channel Fleet'; if true, it perfectly illustrates all that was wrong – the senior officers wanted no harsh interruption of their leisurely existence and had not the imagination to realise the troubles that were simmering beneath the surface. For discontent was rife; it was not organised and it was not, initially, precisely associated with specific ills but it was growing. There was the apparently pointless routine, (it would seem pointless: if a man's seniors set about a duty in a lackadaisical fashion, his obvious deduction is that the duty, in which he is involved, is not very important), there were the obvious injustices and, far, far worse, the growing impression that the government and Admiralty could not care less about the problems of its sailors. The simple and unlettered men who were the victims of the malaise were unable to specify what was wrong, but the general feeling gradually crystallised under the heading of pay. This was, after all, the most glaring and readily definable injustice. In March, a number of men contrived to send a respectfully worded round robin on the subject to Lord Howe. Lord Howe, who was about to hand over formal command to Lord Bridport, passed the complaint on to the Admiralty. The Admiralty did nothing; they did not even tell the new C-in-C, Lord Bridport, that they had received it.

The fleet sailed for a routine cruise and returned at the end of March, when the men realised that their attempt to raise their complaints politely had been met with silence. Not unnaturally, bitterness increased.

Early in April, rumblings of mutiny came to the ears of Lord Bridport, and he learned for the first time of the petition to Lord Howe. Although it does not seem to have occurred to him, or anybody else, to make any representations about it at an earlier and less explosive stage, he was not unsympathetic to the men's case. Now he did take it up with the Admiralty, only to be told to take the fleet to sea. This he attempted to do on 16 April 1797, and the mutiny started. It was the most orderly mutiny imaginable, controlled by delegates from each battleship (frigates, by common agreement, continued their duty of convoy protection). Discipline was maintained and officers continued to receive the courtesies due to their rank; it was made clear that, if the French should put to sea, the mutiny would be postponed. Nevertheless, the situation had worsened. Had there been a half-sympathetic response to the original petition, it is very possible that the whole problem would have passed off without serious disruption, but now additional demands were made – all, however, perfectly reasonable. They were:

A revision of pay.
An end to the practice by pursers of fiddling the ration issue.
An issue of fresh vegetables while in port.

Proper care of the sick and payment to the same until they were discharged.

Shore leave.

These seem to us entirely and self-evidently just. Indeed, they did so to the Board of Enquiry instituted by the Admiralty, but the matter was handled badly. The lesson of the supreme importance of straight dealing had not been fully learned; attempts were made to save face by arguing over details and the attitude of the mutineers hardened. Red flags were flown instead of ensigns and unpopular officers were sent ashore – still however, without violence and without indignity to the officers remaining aboard. At last, however, agreement was reached; the negotiators promised compliance with the men's demands and guaranteed pardons for the delegates. The mutiny was called off and the fleet prepared to sail.

While the fleet waited at St Helens for a favourable wind things began to go wrong. There was bound to be some delay in implementing the authorities' promises because, in many of them, Parliament was involved. During the debates in Parliament, the reported words of politicians, intent on their devious ploys, cast doubt on the government's intentions. The situation was exacerbated by a foolish Admiralty instruction circulated to all captains, which, of course, was leaked to the crews. Intended as a face-saver for senior officials, it was belligerently worded, as though the authorities were still defying the mutineers, instead of preparing to meet their demands. Such influences were enough to upset the fragile calm in the fleet, and when, on 7 May, the wind changed, the men again refused to sail. This time the Admiralty realised that they had got to come clean, quickly and unmistakably. Lord Howe was called from retirement and given full powers to grant pardons and redress grievances. He visited every ship in turn and, having the respect of the men, managed at last to settle matters. The Channel fleet mutiny was now definitely over and it set sail for Brest.

Almost at once, however, a second mutiny broke out in the ships stationed at the Nore which spread to the North Sea Fleet at Yarmouth. This was not the good-tempered affair that the Spithead mutiny had been; it was led by Richard Parker, a misguided man, who was undoubtedly a demagogue more interested in leading a rebellion than in correcting genuine wrongs. The crews no longer had the sympathy of the country behind them, and the mutineers finally mutinied against Parker and returned to their duty. The last ship to do so was *Sandwich* on 15 June 1797, about two months after the first flare-up at Spithead.

Unlike Spithead, where all were pardoned and all voluntarily returned to duty, at the Nore there were a number of ringleaders besides Parker, who desisted from mutiny only because they were made to by the majority. These men were brought to trial. Out of about four hundred, most were pardoned, some were flogged or imprisoned and twenty-eight were hanged. This may be considered a moderate response by the government since, strictly speaking, all mutineers were liable to only one punishment, and that death. On the other hand, even if it had wanted to, the government could not have hanged the whole navy. It is perhaps fair to say that, at the end of the whole unhappy affair, the government behaved with some degree of sense.

The mutinies reveal a great deal about the navy of the time. The first obvious conclusion is that grievances were heartfelt, to have caused the mutinies at all. Of equal importance, however, is that the demands made were so moderate and, significantly, that very little was said about brutalities or hardships. The main demands were all to do with administrative matters concerning the government more than the ships' officers. It was made clear who were the unpopular and therefore probably (although not certainly) the most unsuitable captains, and in the process of reconciliation most of these were removed; in general, however, it was clear that the matter of relations between officers and men was not a major point of contention. The mutineers frequently expressed their loyalty to the country's cause and once normality was restored, the same men sailed away to win the battle of Camperdown and not long afterwards the battle of the Nile.

The conclusion must be that the crews of the fighting ships, pressed men and quota men though they might be, had pride and self-respect, and under proper leadership such men are not unhappy. In the long term the mutinies had the effect of increasing the probability that men were properly led. Not only were some captains removed from posts they were unfit to fill, but the feelings of the common sailor were brought to the attention of a great many people who had never considered such a thing before. The hand of the growing number of enlightened and liberal officers was strengthened, and the vital concept of an officer having a duty towards the men he leads – always

clearly understood by the best – began to be more widely dis-
seminated.

It seems very probable that, after Lord St Vincent and his kind had
improved the effectiveness of the navy, and men like Nelson had
improved its humanity, life was not unendurable. The pleasure and
satisfaction of being part of a successful and well-run unit with good
esprit de corps must not be underrated; it can outweigh a great deal
of hardship, it is what old men of the late twentieth century are
thinking of when they reminisce about the companionship they once
enjoyed, and it is something that those who have never been fortunate
enough to experience it can hardly understand. But it does and did
exist; it is probable that the crews of the ships of the line felt it and
that they were, in essentials, like all servicemen before or since their
time, very ordinary, most of the time cheerful, or at least resigned,
and some of the time heroic.

CHAPTER 4

The Glorious First of June

In wartime it is right and proper that a country should keep up its spirits by putting the best possible light on the actions of its own forces and not dwelling unduly on successes of the enemy. It is, therefore, entirely understandable that the events of the First of June 1794 should have been celebrated by the British as a great victory and dubbed 'Glorious'. After all, in the first major naval battle of the war, seven French ships of the line were taken or sunk and no British ship was lost. Nevertheless, on any realistic basis, it was the French who had, in spite of their losses, achieved a major victory.

France was an agricultural country with a fairly low density of population. She had always been able to grow all the food she needed and foodstuffs formed no part of her seaborne trade. In 1793, however, only a few months after taking on the sea power of Great Britain, the unthinkable happened: the harvest failed. Famine in 1794 became a real possibility. On the borders of France her armies were fighting hard and in the interior there was dissension and resistance to revolutionary measures in a number of quarters. The dissension had been met by the authorities with a campaign of terror which brought fear to everyone. The situation was only just under control and, with famine added, there would be little hope of keeping it so. If supplies were disrupted by internal unrest, the military effort would collapse and, as a result, the Revolution would be brought to an enforced end. If France were to survive, a new source of grain was essential.

Fortunately for her, the one country still in sympathy with the Revolution had supplies to spare. The young republic of America owed its existence to the help given by France to the erstwhile colonial rebels and, from its already substantial resources, French envoys had no difficulty in buying all the grain they needed. By Christmas 1793 a hundred merchant ships had been gathered on America's east coast ready to be loaded with grain. On the other side of the Atlantic, Rear-Admiral Vanstabel was leaving Brest with a small flotilla, the first of the warships which were to convoy them home.

A few years later Vanstabel's chances of getting clear of Brest would have been slim. In 1793, however, the men at the head of the Royal Navy had not yet assimilated the importance to Britain of a close blockade of France; nor had the determination necessary to enforce such a blockade been developed. They still clung to a concept that ships could be preserved for battle by keeping them in harbour. True, occasional stately training cruises were made; these certainly gave opportunity for gunnery practice and sail-handling drills but could not produce the cohering and fining-down effect brought about by hard operational service. It was, at best, defensive not offensive. It was waiting to see what the French would do and then, with luck, countering it, rather than taking the initiative. It meant that most of the time the Channel Fleet was tucked up in Spithead, with only a few frigates at sea to bring back information on French activities. It was usually several, perhaps many, days before such information could be acted upon. So Vanstabel got clean away.

Unhampered by any British initiative, French plans came steadily to fruition in the spring of 1794. In America, the transport of grain to New England ports and the loading of the ships continued. By early April Vanstabel had the convoy assembled in Hampton roads and ready to leave. At the same time a further five ships of the line, under Rear-Admiral Nielly, left Brest intending to meet the returning convoy in mid-Atlantic. Once again the French ships got clean away, unhindered by any action by the British.

There were two effective courses of action open to the British navy. A fleet could have been sent across the Atlantic to wait for the convoy outside American territorial waters, or a close blockade of the French Atlantic ports could have been mounted. In the first case the convoy would not have sailed; in the second it would never have got to France. Neither of these things was done. Men had not yet become accustomed to thinking in terms of total war, and in the eighteenth century, they were slow to recognise civilian starvation as a weapon. However, something of the importance of the convoy was realised and on 2 May the Channel fleet left Spithead under the command of Lord Howe. Even then no great sense of urgency was displayed; the fleet's departure had been held up until a convoy of British merchant ships bound across the Atlantic was ready to depart. Thirty-two ships of the line and ten frigates sailed down the Channel. In the Western Approaches the fleet divided; one-quarter of the warships heading out with the convoy across the Atlantic, and the remaining twenty-six battleships and seven frigates sailing south under the command of Lord Howe. On 5 May Howe arrived off Brest and his frigates, sailing as near to the Goulet de Brest – the harbour entrance – as the shore batteries would permit, reported that the main body of the French fleet was still inside.

There were now three options open to Lord Howe. First, it was obvious that the French fleet would soon be leaving Brest to protect the grain convoy as it approached the shores of France. He could wait until it came out and then bring it to action; with the French fleet defeated he could wait for the convoy and take it at leisure. Alternatively, he could allow the French to come out and then follow discreetly until they led him to the convoy. This would be the most certain way of finding it, after which he would have to defeat the French fleet, at the same time controlling the convoy so that it could not run away while the warships were occupied in battle. His third option was to sail at once and hope he found the grain convoy before the French did.

The first two options assume that the French fleet would easily be defeated. It has to be remembered that Howe could not be sure of this; the last time he had fought the French they had been formidable opponents. In either case, if the defeat of the French were not rapid and total, there would be every chance of losing the convoy. Howe could not have known of the deterioration in the French navy following the Revolution and the possibility of a fudged result must have seemed very strong. He decided on the third option and turned away, out into the Atlantic.

Lord Howe was unlucky. In the days of sail, when freedom of movement was limited and voyages were planned to use prevailing winds, it was often possible to predict fairly accurately the route of a vessel or convoy; Howe had every hope that he would find the grain convoy before the French fleet arrived to reinforce it. Unfortunately he did not. After two weeks of unsuccessful searching, he returned to Brest to find the harbour empty.

The French fleet, including twenty-one ships of the line, had left Brest three days earlier under the command of Admiral Louis Thomas Villaret de Joyeuse. Villaret de Joyeuse was an experienced officer who had been promoted to captain for gallantry in the old royalist navy. Although a royalist, he was no courtier and, at the time of the revolution, felt his duty lay in continuing to serve France. Someone in the revolutionary government had the sense to allow him to do so instead of sending him to the guillotine. He had risen to high rank in consequence, but his situation was now far from enviable. To ensure his best efforts, Villaret de Joyeuse had been told that, should the convoy not arrive safely, his head would be forfeit. At the height of the Terror in France this was no empty threat; to make sure that he did not forget it, a representative of the National Convention, or political commissar, had been appointed to accompany him.

It would have been a brave man who did not feel apprehension as the French fleet sailed out between the dark cliffs which guard the entrance to Brest. Villaret de Joyeuse was no starry-eyed fanatic believing that revolutionary fire in the belly would overcome everything. He was a professional seaman who was well aware of the deficiencies of his command: the men unsettled and undrilled, the officers, for the most part, hastily found and inadequate substitutes for the guillotined professionals. With this force he had to find the grain convoy, perhaps a thousand miles out in the Atlantic, before it was found by the British. Then he had to bring it safely back, fighting off what he knew would be a formidable opposing force. Failure to do so would mean dishonour and the end of France, which, however, would not concern him because before the end came he would be dead.

It was pure chance that on his second day out, Villaret de Joyeuse did not meet the British fleet on its way back. On 18 May, the two fleets cannot have been more than a hundred miles apart and Howe had seven frigates. The principal function of frigates, when accompanying a battle fleet, was reconnaissance. In clear weather vessels could signal to each other over considerable distances. From the masthead, a man with both good eyesight and a good telescope could read flag signals perhaps four or five miles away; in the case of a simple signal such as letting the fore topsail fly in the wind, certainly ten miles or more. Therefore, a few vessels sailing in line abreast could cover a band of ocean ten or more times as many miles wide as the number of vessels involved.

Lord Howe would not have wished to spread out his line-of-battle ships in this manner because of the time it would take to get them back together in the event of meeting an enemy force, and in any case that is what frigates were for. Frigates were not required to engage ships of the line – the disparity of force was too great – and ships of the line did not fire on frigates in a general engagement unless the frigate fired first. Consequently, by sending his frigates far afield, an admiral did not weaken his force. All this means that Lord Howe could keep observation on a belt of sea seventy miles wide. Nevertheless, the two fleets did not meet and Villaret de Joyeuse got clear away.

A few years later, Nelson was to say that 'want of frigates' would be found engraved on his heart. Battle fleets never had enough frigates. If there had been more in Lord Howe's fleet, he might well have met Villaret de Joyeuse. Better still, he could have left a couple off Brest after his first visit. He might then have received early warning of the French departure. The direction they took would have given a clue to the path of the convoy and, if the frigate with the message had been quick enough, Howe might still have got to the convoy first. As it was, he did not get early warning, nor did he encounter the French outward bound. His only intimation of their movements was the empty harbour he found when he got back to Brest.

On 19 May he turned away for the second time and resumed his search of the empty sea. Empty it remained for a further nine days. As the dawn broke on the morning of 28 May 1794, it looked as empty as in all the previous dawns and perhaps even greyer than usual. The fleet was about four hundred miles west of Ushant, sailing south-east on yet another sweep between the approaches to the Irish Sea and the Bay of Biscay. The sky was cloudy and the wind was fresh from the SSW. The pulse of the masthead lookout on Howe's flagship, *Queen Charlotte*, may have quickened when, at 5 a.m., he saw a signal hoist break out from the mizzen-mast of *Latona*, one of the frigates sailing ahead of the fleet. On the other hand perhaps it didn't: there had been many false alarms during the search for Villaret. In fact, after three hours of suspense, this sighting proved to be another false alarm, the sail being a merchant brig bound for London. However, no sooner had this fact been established by the frigates than further sails were seen to the south. This time there was little doubt. It was the French fleet at last.

The fleet, when first seen, was about fifteen miles to the south. It was indeed that of Villaret de Joyeuse, who had linked up with Nielly, bringing his command up to twenty-six ships of the line. He had met the grain convoy which was further out in the Atlantic, heading eastward for Brest. He was cruising at large, well ahead of it and, at the moment of sighting was sailing roughly north, with the SSW wind behind him, directly towards Lord Howe's fleet.

Almost at once the French turned westward, forming a line of battle on the larboard tack. They settled to a course roughly north-west, heading back to the convoy, and nearer to Howe although not directly towards him. It would have made no sense to seek an immediate battle; if the British won (and Villaret had no illusions), they would be handed the convoy on a plate. Neither did Villaret want to turn away; Lord Howe might then ignore him and go in search of the grain ships. By heading north-west he was trailing his coat, not rushing, bull-headed, into trouble but inviting Howe to bring him to action by tacking to windward.

Lord Howe flew the signal to tack. This brought his fleet hard on the wind on the larboard tack, heading about West by North; Villaret was sailing free, heading about north-west. Their paths would eventually cross but Villaret had the initiative; he could, at any time, turn downwind towards the British, he could keep going as he was, or, whenever he wished, he could turn about and sail away south-east with a commanding lead over any pursuit.

By mid-afternoon the two fleets on their converging courses were drawing rapidly together. Villaret shortened sail from time to time, to make sure that he did not get ahead of the British line of advance. It was clear that Lord Howe would soon order another tack, which would turn him directly towards the French, and Villaret now gave the order to turn away to the south-east. As his fleet did so the foremost British ships arrived almost within gunshot range and, by the time the French rear was turning, shots were being exchanged.

The timing was exactly right: by the time his turn was complete the hunt was in full cry, Lord Howe was hooked in pursuit and Villaret was off and running. Every moment took both fleets further and further away from the precious convoy. Lord Howe had signalled 'General Chase', which meant that every ship was to sail as fast as it could in pursuit and never mind formation.

By now the wind was fresh and squally and Howe's ships were cramming on sail in headlong pursuit of the flying enemy. As overloaded sails and gear gave way under the strain, they were replaced faster than they ever had been at drill in the Channel. It is doubtful if anyone in the entire fleet gave a thought to the grain convoy, now *en route* to pass well to the rear. At about 8 p.m. the 74-gun *Audacious*

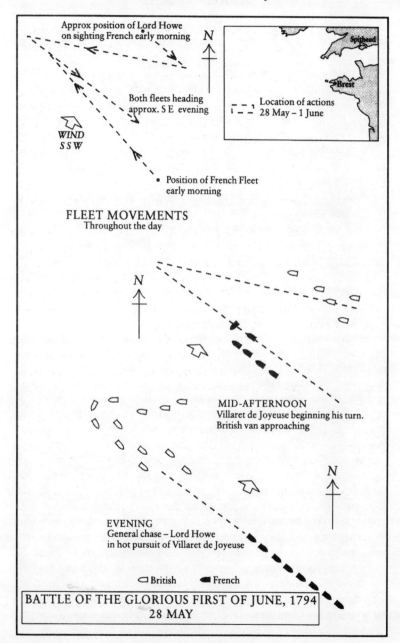

Approx position of Lord Howe
on sighting French early morning

N

Location of actions
28 May – 1 June

Spithead

Brest

Both fleets heading
approx. S E evening

WIND
S S W

• Position of French Fleet
early morning

FLEET MOVEMENTS
Throughout the day

N

MID-AFTERNOON
Villaret de Joyeuse beginning his turn.
British van approaching

N

EVENING
General chase – Lord Howe
in hot pursuit of Villaret de Joyeuse

British   French

BATTLE OF THE GLORIOUS FIRST OF JUNE, 1794
28 MAY

caught up with the 110-gun *Révolutionnaire*. Broadsides had been exchanged at some distance between *Révolutionnaire* and other ships but *Audacious* came close alongside. For nearly two hours in the darkening evening the two ships slogged it out, with a strengthening wind moaning in their rigging and the grey sea sluicing between their hulls. Now the higher standard of training in the British ship began to pay off; she had not been worked as hard as the navy would be worked later in the war but she was controlled by professional officers and petty officers who had drilled the crew in gunnery and sail-handling both in harbour and at sea. The French were still suffering from the upheavals of the Revolution and from an over-long sojourn in Brest. They had virtually no experience of handling guns on moving decks. Thus it was that a 74-gun ship was able successfully to take on one of 110 guns. Just before 10 p.m. *Révolutionnaire*, almost simultaneously, struck her colours, lost her mizzen-mast and ran into *Audacious*. *Audacious*, however, had been fought almost to a standstill. The damage to her rigging was so great 'as to render the ship entirely ungovernable' and she could not take possession of the surrendered *Révolutionnaire*. The two ships drifted apart. By the following morning *Audacious* had cobbled together a rig of sorts but could only sail before the wind; in this condition she would not even risk action with the frigates which had come back to succour *Révolutionnaire*. All she could do was to make for home, which she reached eight days later.

Meanwhile, the two fleets continued their wild chase through the stormy night. At dawn on the 29th, *Audacious* was nowhere to be seen; both fleets were sailing south-east, the French being in line and about five miles to windward. At some time during the night, while the British had been trying to achieve maximum speed, the French had regained their windward advantage. Lord Howe called his fleet to order by flying the signals to end the chase and form line of battle. The two lines of ships continued on their way, the British being to leeward (to the north) of the French and partly overlapping their line.

At about 7 a.m. Lord Howe flew the signal to tack in succession, which meant that the British line was now heading west towards the tail of the French, losing ground in a forwards direction but making good the five miles which had been lost to leeward. After observing this manoeuvre for a little while, Villaret de Joyeuse ordered his line to wear and retrace its track. The British movement was a reminder that they might lose interest in chasing him and turn about to seek

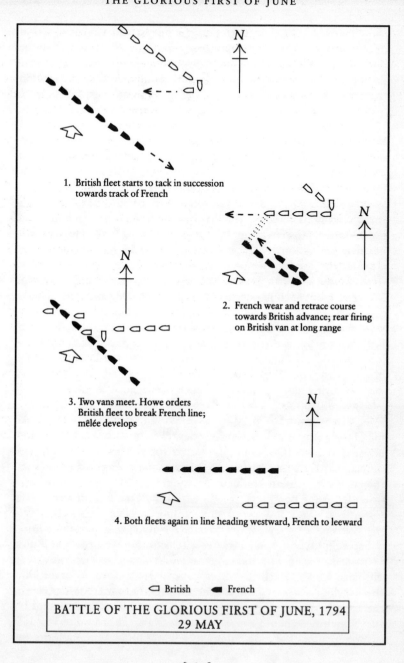

1. British fleet starts to tack in succession towards track of French

2. French wear and retrace course towards British advance; rear firing on British van at long range

3. Two vans meet. Howe orders British fleet to break French line; mêlée develops

4. Both fleets again in line heading westward, French to leeward

◁ British   ◀ French

BATTLE OF THE GLORIOUS FIRST OF JUNE, 1794
29 MAY

the convoy; it was his clear duty to keep them too occupied to do so. Now the British were sailing west and the French roughly north-west, the two fleets drawing steadily closer to each other. The French rear had opened fire at long range as they drew away from the path of the British, and now the French van was beginning to fire at an ever-decreasing range as it approached.

The situation began to take on the appearance of a traditional battle between lines of ships, each ship commencing operations as its opponent came up. Lord Howe knew that, with twenty-five or -six ships in each line, such a battle was not likely to be decisive; furthermore, he was in the leeward position. There were arguments for and against fighting from the leeward position, but there was no doubt that the admiral in the windward position at the start of a battle held the initiative. Howe was not yet ready to give away the initiative and he took the action which would make sure he kept it. Instead of allowing the line battle to develop, he made signals requiring his ships to tack and break the enemy's line; instead of gradually drawing nearer to the French his ships were to turn towards and pass through them. The result was a general mêlée, at the end of which both fleets were again in line of battle, but this time with the French to leeward. Both fleets were on the larboard tack which, since the wind remained roughly SSW throughout all encounters, meant that both fleets were heading in a generally western direction. They were both preoccupied with repairing damage and the French fleet tended to fall further off to leeward.

The night of the 29–30 May passed without incident but the morning of the 30th brought an entirely new element into the drama – fog, unusual because the wind was still strong. The British fleet was moving slowly west, still on the larboard tack, engaged on repairs; the enemy was totally hidden. At about 10 a.m. the fog lifted sufficiently for the two fleets to sight each other; the French were to the north-west – still downwind – but sailing east. As soon as they saw the British fleet they tacked to come round on a parallel course. Villaret de Joyeuse had turned east to look for the British and now he turned to keep with them; he no more wanted to lose touch than did Lord Howe. The British fleet was ordered to form up and follow the flagship; *Queen Charlotte* turned slightly to starboard towards the French. Almost at once the fog began to thicken and by midday the French fleet had disappeared from sight. Shortly afterwards it became opaque and no ship could see any other. Although the fog was thick the wind remained strong; it was obviously impossible to continue the attack and there was real danger of collisions between ships within the British fleet. All that could be done was to turn back to the original course, and shorten sail to keep minimum steerage way, while listening for sound signals from nearby ships.

Conditions stayed much the same for the next twenty-four hours. Nothing was seen of the French fleet but occasionally the fog would lift enough for one or two British ships to be seen. It was not until early afternoon of Saturday, 31 May that the fog cleared and normal operations could be resumed. The French could be seen about five or six miles downwind to the north and the British ships which had become separated closed on the flagship. It was dusk before all ships were back in formation and throughout the night the fleet kept up a slow progress to westward while the frigates maintained a watch on the French.

The dawn of Sunday, 1 June 1794 came with a cloudy sky and a fresh wind from the south. Lord Howe's fleet continued to sail slowly to the west and the French kept on a roughly parallel course to leeward. At last the scene was set, there were no further complications and the two antagonists were in their corners waiting for the bell. Lord Howe lined up his fleet directly to windward of the French and flew the signal announcing his intention to pass through the enemy line. This meant that his ships would have to endure enemy fire from ahead as they approached, but would be able, as they passed through the enemy line, to fire devastating broadsides into the vulnerable bows and sterns of the ships they were passing. Thereafter they would bring up opposite their opponents' lee sides; they would be in the worst of the gunsmoke but the enemy would not be able to escape. A ship in the midst of battle could turn away quite readily downwind, even with damaged rigging, but to turn away upwind would be much more difficult and require much more preparation. Therefore a ship in the upwind position had to fight or surrender; there was little chance of her running away. Lord Howe wanted a decisive battle from which no enemy could escape, so he chose to go through the French line.

The French had no intention of avoiding action; if ever a man went into battle with a song in his heart, it must have been Louis Villaret de Joyeuse. For five days he had led the British fleet away from the precious grain convoy, and when he could lead them no further he had brought them to battle; he had done all that could possibly be expected of him and the convoy must, by now, be well out of harm's

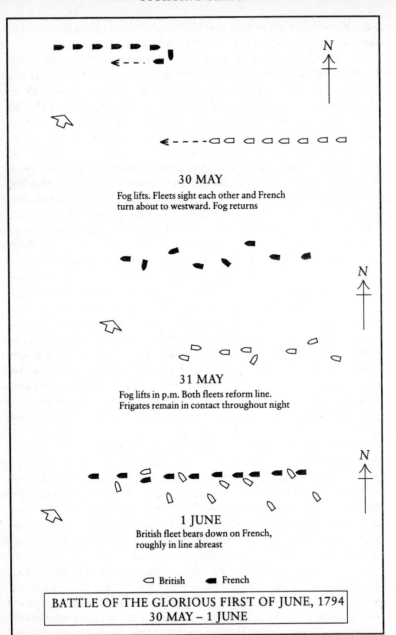

30 MAY

Fog lifts. Fleets sight each other and French
turn about to westward. Fog returns

31 MAY

Fog lifts in p.m. Both fleets reform line.
Frigates remain in contact throughout night

1 JUNE

British fleet bears down on French,
roughly in line abreast

◁ British ◀ French

**BATTLE OF THE GLORIOUS FIRST OF JUNE, 1794
30 MAY – 1 JUNE**

way. Whatever the outcome of the battle, he had succeeded; he was safe from dishonour and a shameful death.

The British fleet bore down in line abreast or approximately so. Lord Howe's intention was that the attackers should arrive at the enemy line simultaneously, run through the line, inflicting raking broadsides as they did so, and round up with each ship on the lee side of her opponent. The French would then be pinned down, unable to break off action and virtually doomed to total defeat. In practice, it proved impossible for twenty-five ships to maintain an orderly line when running downwind side by side and suffering damage from enemy fire. Consequently those French ships which were not attacked immediately had time to move to the assistance of those who were, and the orderly plan became considerably disrupted. Another difficulty was that there were still ambiguities in the signal code; it had not yet been printed and each ship had a hand-made copy. In particular, the all-important signal no. 34 (to pass through the enemy's line) could be interpreted either as mandatory or as a general intention which could be varied by individual ships according to circumstances. It was not an easy manoeuvre to perform in a brisk wind and there were circumstances in which it might appear impracticable, for example, if two ships closed the gap between the bow of one and the stern of the other. (At Trafalgar, in such circumstances, Nelson just crashed through, but this spirited behaviour had not yet become the standard. In fairness, it must be said that at Trafalgar the wind was light, whereas Howe's ships were in a brisk breeze.) Consequently, rather less than half of Howe's ships actually succeeded in breaking through.

The battle became more of a mêlée than intended and the French eventually managed to withdraw to leeward but not before great punishment was taken by both sides. The most celebrated incident of the battle was the duel between *Brunswick* and *Vengeur*, both 74s. *Brunswick* had gone straight through the French line and came to alongside *Vengeur* so closely that their anchors locked; neither ship could manoeuvre and there was no option for either except a brutal slogging match at point-blank range until one of them should yield. After four hours, and in a sinking condition, *Vengeur* struck her flag; her masts went overboard shortly afterwards. The two ships disentangled themselves; *Brunswick*, although for the moment completely disabled, still had two masts standing and was blown bodily downwind. *Vengeur*, with all masts gone and settling lower in the water, wallowed sullenly where she was. Before any assistance could be given, *Brunswick* found herself to leeward of the main body of the French, who were beginning to regroup. Too disabled to continue any action, all she could do was sail to leeward until sufficiently far from the French to start making repairs; she eventually succeeded in reaching Spithead eleven days later. *Albert*, which, although much damaged, was able to set some sail, was ordered to take possession of *Vengeur*. As she approached it became obvious that nothing could be done except hoist out all boats to save as many as possible of the crew. Two hundred and thirteen men were taken aboard *Albert* before *Vengeur* went down with the rest. Much was made of the contest in France, where it was reported that *Vengeur* sank in battle with guns firing and the crew shouting 'Vive la République!' As with all legends the truth is less highly coloured, but in this case it was impressive enough.

Because the penetration of the French line had been less than was intended, Villaret de Joyeuse was able to withdraw to leeward in comparatively good order, although he left six ships in British hands. The British ships were in need of a good deal of running repairs before there could be any thought of renewing the battle. It may be thought that the grain convoy's position could have been discovered from some of the many prisoners taken that day, and a further effort made to catch it, but this did not happen. Perhaps it was considered that the convoy was already too far away to be caught, perhaps there was not a sufficient force in an adequate state of repair or perhaps nobody was thinking straight. No modern battle conditions are quite comparable with those in sea battles between wooden ships. Against most modern weapons, a man is either keeping his head down under cover or dead; by the time the First of June was over the participants had been engaged on grindingly hard physical labour for twelve or fifteen hours, much of it within a few yards of the mouths of thirty or forty cannon. At the end of that time, one did not think too clearly about what to do next, one collapsed; and this was largely true of the captains and admirals as well. If they had not had the physical labour, they had been under intense mental strain and they had all been in the same conditions of danger as their men. It is not surprising if they felt they had done all that could be expected. Certainly the country thought so: when Lord Howe and his men returned to Portsmouth they were greeted as heroes. Bonfires were lit and bells were rung in celebration of a glorious victory. It was a not ignoble reaction. People still thought that wars were for fighting men, and the fact that these men had failed to bring starvation to French civilians did not worry them at all.

As for Louis Thomas Villaret de Joyeuse, it is pleasing to record that he survived the Terror and although, because of his royalist sympathies he did come under a cloud for a while, it was lifted under Napoleon and he ended his days in some dignity as governor of Venice.

CHAPTER 5

Spaniards, Ireland and Cape St Vincent

Spain, on which France had declared war in 1793, found herself obliged by internal instability to make peace in 1795. A year later, the victim of politicians, she was in alliance with France against Great Britain. It was not a popular step either with the entrenched nobility or with the people who, whatever the shortcomings of their own ruling circles, had no great love for the French Revolution.

Twelve years later, when Napoleon tried to take military control, there was a remarkable resurgence of spirit in Spain, but in 1796 the Spaniards were not enthusiastic about either Britain or France. The Spanish navy, which was now at the disposal of France, was not in good condition and the French authorities were not qualified to be of any help in improving it. However, it was of considerable size, and the first effect of the new alliance, as far as Britain was concerned, was that the number of hostile ships in the Mediterranean was more than doubled. This fact, together with the loss of usable ports, obliged the British navy to leave the Mediterranean at the end of 1796, and the acquisition of a theoretically powerful fleet caused the French to think about the possibility of direct action against the British Isles.

As Napoleon himself was to confirm a year later, there was little hope, at that time, of mounting a full-scale invasion of England, but what did seem practicable was to foment an insurrection in Ireland. The curse which has plagued Britain's relations with Ireland for five hundred years was in full operation: the Irish were poor, hungry and incompetently governed by the British, who compounded that incompetence by providing far too small a garrison to keep the angry population in check. Much of the British army had been wasted on taking and holding French islands in the West Indies, which satisfied only the newspapers and some commercial interests. It did little to harm the French, and nothing at all for the stability of Ireland, where those Irishmen who were not away in the ranks of Britain's best fighting regiments were in a state of seething rebellion. One of the principal leaders of the rebel movement was a young lawyer, Theobald Wolfe Tone. He was a fervent advocate of direct action, and the French Revolution, with its declaration of liberty, equality and fraternity for all, seemed the embodiment of all his hopes. If an invasion by the French were combined with an open revolt by the Irish, a free Ireland could, he thought, be a real possibility instead of a remote ideal. The French were happy to nourish this dream, and when, in February 1796, Tone arrived (via America) in Paris, he was welcomed and given a commission as an adjutant-general in the French army.

Ten months later, in the winter of 1796-7, Tone's dream came true to the extent that an attempt against Ireland was made. It took place against a background of a succession of accidents and failures which afflicted both sides; on the whole the French came out of it with more credit than the British, who did not perform to the high standard they reached later in the wars.

In the autumn of 1796 as events turned against Britain, Admiral Sir John Jervis, with a fleet of fifteen ships of the line off Toulon, was hard pressed. There was a potential enemy fleet of forty ships in the Mediterranean. Napoleon was advancing in northern Italy, and the number of harbours available to the Royal Navy was dwindling. Yet there was still hope; seven ships of the line under Admiral Robert Man were on their way to join Sir John, and with twenty-two ships available, the grim old man would have a good chance of defeating any Franco-Spanish fleet he was likely to meet. A dramatic victory would hearten some of the smaller states opposing Napoleon and might lead to his conquests being less complete; it could even enable the navy to maintain its position in the Mediterranean. But any such hopes were lost in almost farcical circumstances.

Admiral Man duly reported to Jervis, but, incredibly, he had not made sure that his ships were properly provisioned for service, without support, in the Mediterranean. Ships were no use to Jervis in an unready state, and he had no alternative but to send them back to Gibraltar, to take on the necessary stores. Man encountered a substantial Spanish fleet on his way to Gibraltar, and was fortunate to arrive there with all his ships intact. In the light of this experience, he decided that the opposition in the Mediterranean was too strong, and that he

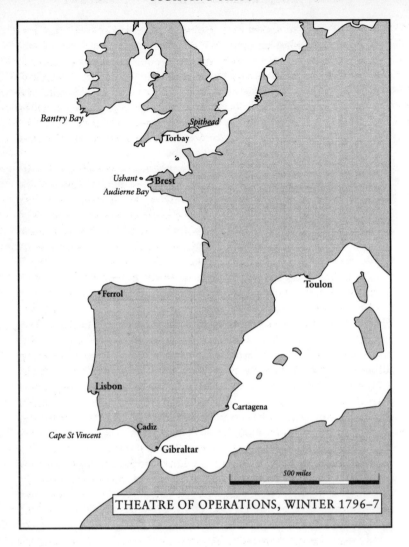

THEATRE OF OPERATIONS, WINTER 1796–7

would do better to return to England and live to fight another day. Without more ado, he took his ships home. Forty years earlier the unfortunate Admiral Byng had been court-martialled and shot for less, but, as Mahan says, 'men were becoming more merciful' and Man's only fate was a reproving letter from the Admiralty and the loss of his command. Sir John Jervis, however, was left without the extra support which could have made all the difference, and withdrawal by the Royal Navy from the Mediterranean became inevitable.

Jervis, in *Victory*, left Toulon with his fleet and sailed for Gibraltar. As soon as he had left the scene a fleet of five French and twenty-seven Spanish ships of the line under the Admiral Pierre Villeneuve, left Toulon bound for Brest. Wolfe Tone's scheme for taking Ireland had been adopted, and Villeneuve's orders were to link up with a French fleet in Brest. The ships gathering at Brest would provide strong naval support to an expedition against Ireland. Villeneuve was not a lucky man and was, perhaps, too straightforward to cope with the politicians who ordered his movements. He was not an inspired admiral, but he deserved better of fate than the series of calamities which befell him, ending in his lonely death in a Rennes hotel room after defeat at Trafalgar. Misfortune struck less than a week after leaving Toulon; the Spaniards decided that they had to go into Cartagena, leaving Villeneuve and his five ships to go on without them. Villeneuve might very well have been intercepted at Gibraltar by Jervis, but in this respect, at least, he was fortunate. An easterly gale – locally called a levanter – swept him through the straits, at the same time preventing the British ships from leaving Gibraltar harbour. Not only did it stop them leaving but it damaged three of Jervis's ships and wrecked a fourth – accidents which should not have happened, although they were the result of inadequate supplies rather than bad seamanship. East winds prevailed all round the western coasts of Europe and Villeneuve got to Brest to find that the expedition he had been ordered to join had already left.

The expedition, commanded by Admiral Morard de Galles, including seventeen ships of the line and troopships for 15,000 men, had been waiting in Camaret roads at the entrance to Brest for a suitable opportunity to leave. A strong east wind gave them their best chance of getting clear and evading the blockading ships outside; on 16 December 1796 Morard de Galles had decided to wait no longer for Villeneuve, but to go at once.

Morard de Galles could have got clear away. The blockade of Brest was not executed by the British with the rigour which would become the norm later in the war. Then, an inshore squadron would have been hanging on like grim death to its station off Ushant, whatever the conditions, with the rest of the fleet not far away. As it was, in conditions ideal for blowing the French out of Brest, the inshore squadron, under Admiral Sir John Colpoys, had sagged off to leeward, well out into the Atlantic. The main body of the British fleet, which should have been at instant readiness, was sheltering in Spithead, whence it had no chance of getting out in an easterly gale. One frigate alone, *Indefatigable* under Sir Edward Pellew, was resolutely holding its station inshore, close to Brest.

In fact, the way out of Brest to the open sea was wide open. Had Morard de Galles stood boldly out to sea, taking the most direct and safest route, he would have encountered nothing but frigates, which could have been brushed aside by his ships of the line. Even if Colpoys had been on station, his battleships would have been about twenty miles offshore; dusk was approaching, and in the stormy conditions of a long winter night, the French fleet would have had a very good chance of getting clear without serious damage.

Almost certainly the result would have been better than what actually happened. Having left the Camaret roads, Morard de Galles changed his mind about the route to be taken through the rocks and shoals which surround the approach to Brest, and confusion inevitably followed. Nightfall increased the confusion, and it was turned into chaos by the spirited action of Sir Edward Pellew.

Sir Edward spent the night sailing through the disorganised French fleet, aping French night signals by firing an occasional gun, showing a variety of lights, burning flares. This destroyed any hope de Galles had of reforming his fleet into any kind of order. By the morning one ship had been driven on to the rocks, and many of the fleet had scattered downwind into the Atlantic, including the frigate *Fraternité* carrying both Morard de Galles and the commander of the troops, General Lazare Hoche. Eight ships, including *Fraternité*, failed to rejoin but the remainder, to their great credit, persisted in their objective and in four days covered the three hundred stormy miles to Ireland. By 21 December 1796 they had arrived off Bantry Bay in Ireland's extreme south-west.

Bantry Bay is more like a very large inlet than a bay as generally understood, being twenty miles long and about three miles wide. The only point where a landing could have been made was at the head of the inlet near the town of Bantry. Now the easterly gales, which had got the French out of Brest and provided a fair wind to Ireland, became their implacable enemy; the head of Bantry Bay lay dead to windward, and the bay was not wide enough for the unpractised French to make progress by tacking. They tried; with their untrained crews and their 15,000 seasick passengers, they tried over and over again to get up the bay. With supplies running out and crews exhausted, one by one the ships had to give up and return to Brest. The last left on 3 January 1797.

Pellew had sent word of the situation to Falmouth but nothing much happened. Instead of staying in the Western Approaches, whence he could have readily moved to any part of the west coast of Britain on receipt of a message, Admiral Colpoys had returned to Spithead for orders. Admiral Lord Bridport, with the main body of the Channel fleet, was still in Spithead where, having failed to get out against the easterly gales, he stayed until the day the French left Ireland.

The French were certainly unlucky in failing to land in Ireland in spite of their prodigious efforts; even in winter it is unusual for gales to blow from the east for such a prolonged period. In not losing Ireland the British were luckier than they deserved; Lord Howe, the nominal C-in-C of the Channel fleet, had displayed his ability in battle two and a half years before; but he was an elderly man in failing health. He had not grasped the importance of a close blockade, nor had he, now, the energy to instil into his subordinates the determination that was required. Bridport and Colpoys were capable men but they did not possess the quality which inspires maximum effort, even in the dull routine of the blockade. Jervis and Nelson did possess it and the standard they set was to become the norm within the British navy but their time had not yet come.

Meanwhile, it was left to the frigates *Indefatigable* and *Amazon* to display the spirit required, when they encountered the French first-rate *Droits de l'Homme* on her way back from Ireland to Brest. Although either frigate could have been reduced to matchwood by one broadside from *Droits de l'Homme*, they succeeded, by determined and immaculate ship-handling, in driving her to destruction in the surf of Audierne Bay.

While the French expedition was coming to its cold and cheerless conclusion, Jervis, to encourage Britain's last beleaguered allies, the

Portuguese, had taken his fleet to Lisbon. Here a fifth ship was lost to him by an accident in the Tagus. By 18 January 1797, he had stationed himself with his ten remaining ships of the line off Cape St Vincent, where he would be likely to intercept any enemy ships heading for the channel or the French north-western ports. Here he was joined by five more ships sent from Spithead to reinforce him. He now had under his command some of the captains who were to set the navy a new standard of excellence, including Foley, Miller, Collingwood, Saumarez, Troubridge and Berry. He was soon to be joined by Nelson, then a commodore, who had been organising the evacuation of the troops from the island of Elba to Gibraltar.

The Directory, as the French government was now called, had not given up hope of amassing, at Brest, a combined fleet sufficiently large to overwhelm any British opposition to a further attempt at Ireland. On 1 February 1797 the Spanish fleet which, three months before, had started out from Toulon with Villeneuve, finally left Cartagena under Admiral Don José de Córdoba. It included twenty-seven ships of the line, twelve frigates and a number of merchant vessels which were to be convoyed as far as Cadiz. The potential danger to Britain was substantial: if the French, Dutch and Spanish fleets could be brought together in the Western Approaches, they would amount to perhaps sixty ships of the line, against which the British could have mustered a theoretical maximum of forty. This superiority of numbers would have outweighed any inferiority of skill. The job of the Royal Navy was, of course, to prevent such a combination, and Jervis at least was in the right position to stop the Spaniards.

Competent action makes its own good fortune. Jervis, denied the Mediterranean, had, in spite of his lost ships, scorned to remain sheltered in the Tagus, and had taken station in the most effective place available. Here, fate brought the Spaniards to him.

After passing through the Straits of Gibraltar, the Spaniards should have had an easy day's sail to Cadiz, and Jervis would have waited at Cape St Vincent in vain. However, as they emerged into the Atlantic, the Spaniards encountered easterly gales. Strong contrary winds were always trouble for sailing warships, since even the limited progress of tacking to windward was not possible in strong winds and rough seas. The best that the most skilfully handled ship could do was avoid being blown too far to leeward; for a ship with a weak or inexperienced crew, the only recourse was to run before the gale. With minimum sail set, to give the ship steerage way, this was easier than fighting the gale, and provided comparative safety at the cost of being blown a long way off course. Admiral Córdoba had charge of five merchant ships which were in poor condition and very short of manpower. All they could do was run before the wind and their naval escort had no choice but to do the same. By the time the wind abated and came round to the west, the Spaniards were hundreds of miles away from Cadiz and their way back was past Jervis's fleet.

In the early morning of 14 February 1797, Sir John in his flagship *Victory*, with fourteen other ships of the line and seven smaller vessels, was on his station about thirty miles south-west of Cape St Vincent; Nelson had joined and had transferred his commodore's broad pennant to the 74-gun ship *Captain* (Captain Ralph Miller). Visibility was hazy, the west wind was light and the fleet was sailing slowly south-east, dipping majestically through the swell. As dawn broke and visibility improved a little, signal flags began to appear at the mastheads of outlying ships reporting the sighting of strange sails ahead. Admiral Córdoba could have turned his misfortune to good account and, having been blown so far west, taken some of his ships north to Ferrol, some eight hundred miles nearer to where he was eventually wanted; but he did not. He took the whole of his fleet back to Cadiz and, in consequence, had been found by Jervis.

Visibility was not only hazy but patchy, and the full extent of the Spanish fleet was only gradually revealed. This gave rise to the story of the numbers being reported to Jervis as he was walking his quarterdeck:

'There are eight sail of the line, Sir John.'
'Very well, sir.'
'There are twenty sail of the line, Sir John.'
'Very well, sir.'
'There are twenty-five sail of the line, Sir John.'
'Very well, sir.'
'There are twenty-seven sail of the line, Sir John.'
'Enough, sir. If there are fifty sail of the line, I shall go through them.'

It is a good story, and consistent with the character of Sir John Jervis; unfortunately it is unlikely that the exchanges were quite so crisp. Ships signalled back what they saw when they saw it; the information received by *Victory* was not quite so tidily progressive and came through over a period of about an hour. It is perfectly true, however, that Sir John would not have been too worried about the odds; he knew his ships, he knew the Spaniards, and his determination would not have been very much influenced by arithmetic.

The Spanish fleet was sailing roughly west to east. On the approach of the British ships out of the north, they appeared to make some effort to form a line of battle, but it was not a very good effort; there was a considerable gap between a group of ships to the leeward, or east, end of the line, and a larger group of ships to the west. The twelve frigates in the Spanish fleet were widely dispersed, and some were convoying the merchant ships to Cadiz on a route further south; the Spanish ships of the line were doing their duty, and protecting their convoy. Jervis ordered the British fleet to form line of battle 'as convenient', which was done with *Victory* near the centre, *Culloden* leading and *Captain* third from the rear. There followed signals adjusting the direction of the line's advance, ordering that the enemy were to be engaged, and that the admiral's intention was to pass through the enemy's line. In their context, they were instructions to the line, led by *Culloden*, to pass through the gap between the two parts of the enemy's fleet and to engage as possible when doing do. By this manoeuvre Jervis was, temporarily at least, reducing the odds to 20:15 since seven of the twenty-seven Spanish ships were in the group to leeward; to give any support to their main body, the leeward group would have to tack or wear and then beat upwind, which would take time. The British fleet bore down heading SSW, and the Spaniards to windward turned to head NNE so that, as the first broadsides were exchanged, Jervis's line and the twenty Spanish windward ships were passing each other on opposite courses about seven or eight hundred yards apart. The leeward group also turned northwards, and did indeed make an attempt to link up with their compatriots. One got through the rear of the British line and succeeded, but the remainder sheered off after two broadsides from *Victory* and took no further part in the action.

As the van of the British line passed the rear of the Spaniards, ignoring for the moment the group to leeward, Jervis ordered the line to tack. This meant turning in succession, each ship following in the wake of the one ahead, towards the Spanish main body and following them on the same course. In other words, the British line, now heading NNE, would gradually catch up with the Spaniards until they were alongside each other and battle would be joined between the two lines. The snag was that, long before the ships at the head of the British line caught up with the leading Spaniards, the British rear, still

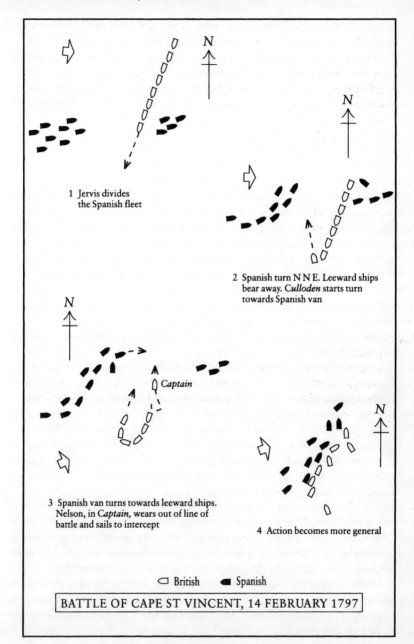

1 Jervis divides
the Spanish fleet

2 Spanish turn N N E. Leeward ships
bear away. *Culloden* starts turn
towards Spanish van

Captain

3 Spanish van turns towards leeward ships.
Nelson, in *Captain,* wears out of line of
battle and sails to intercept

4 Action becomes more general

British   Spanish

BATTLE OF CAPE ST VINCENT, 14 FEBRUARY 1797

on its SSW course, would be well past them. There would then be nothing to prevent the Spanish van turning east to link up with the leeward group, which would nullify the advantage Jervis had gained by dividing the Spanish fleet.

It was now that Nelson made a move which has passed into legend. Appreciating that the Spanish leading ship, the 120-gun *Santísima Trinidad*, was turning towards the leeward group, he ordered Captain Miller to leave the line of battle, wear round and intercept her. This was successfully done; the leading Spanish ships were forced to turn to windward and slow down, with the result that the British ships caught up more quickly, and the action became general. The Spanish ships to leeward made no further effort to join battle.

While Nelson in *Captain* was making his turn, Jervis supported his action by flying the signal for 'each ship to take suitable station and engage as arriving up in succession', which meant that each captain was freed from the restraint of the line and could get into action as quickly and effectively as possible. Captain Troubridge, in *Culloden* at the van of the British line, responded by ignoring the Spanish rear and pressing forward to support Nelson, while Collingwood in *Excellent* followed him out of the line to get to his aid as soon as possible. By mid-afternoon two Spanish first-rates and two 74s had surrendered; the remainder got clear and stayed clear.

Leaving the line has been described as a daring indiscipline, carried out by Nelson at the risk of disgrace for disobeying orders, but this is over-dramatizing the event. Certainly the *Fighting Instructions*, then in force, expressly forbade any captain, however hard-pressed, to leave the line in order to avoid the heat of the action; they did not say, however, that a senior officer must never use his initiative. Indeed, a senior officer in any force could be held very much at fault, if he lost an opportunity for effective action because there was not time to seek permission from his superior. Nelson did the right thing; he stands alone and does not need commendation for daringly breaking the letter of the rules.

Certainly the battle set Nelson on the road to fame. *Captain*, having headed off *Santísima Trinidad*, became, in company with *Culloden*, heavily engaged with the 112-gun *San José* and the 80-gun *San Nicolás*. *Culloden* became crippled and fell astern, leaving *Captain* momentarily alone and under heavy fire, with sails and rigging badly damaged. She was given a few minutes' respite by *Excellent* moving forward, between her and *San Nicolás*. Under fire from *Excellent*,

1 *Culloden* and *Captain* engage *St José* and *San Nicolás*

2 *Culloden*, disabled, falls away. *Captain* on her own but *Excellent* approaching

3 *Excellent* moves alongside *San Nicolás*. *Captain* damaged but still with steerageway. Mizzen-mast of *San José* destroyed

4 *Excellent* moves forward. *San José* falls against *San Nicolás*. With last of steerageway *Captain* turns into *San Nicolás* and boards both

NELSON'S PATENT BRIDGE FOR BOARDING FIRST-RATES

San Nicolás turned upwind at a moment when, suddenly unbalanced by the loss of her mizzen-mast, *San José* fell downwind; *Excellent* moved ahead and the two Spanish ships collided, becoming inextricably locked together. *Captain* had just lost her last sail and her wheel had been shot away, but Nelson ordered Captain Miller to put her helm over (by manhandling the great tiller normally controlled by ropes from the wheel), and the last of her steerage way put her alongside *San Nicolás*. Captain Berry who was temporarily a supernumary on board, and soldiers of the 69th Regiment who were acting as Marines on *Captain*, promptly boarded *San Nicolás*; they were closely followed by Nelson, who ordered Captain Miller to stay. While receiving the surrender of *San Nicolás*, the boarding party were fired on from *San José* locked alongside; so they moved on and boarded her in turn. Nelson received the swords of the officers of both ships on the quarterdeck of *San José*. The incident caught the imagination of the fleet, and *San Nicolás* was referred to as 'Nelson's patent bridge for boarding first-rates'.

On the following morning the British fleet sailed slowly into Lagos Bay (on the Portuguese south coast about twenty miles east of Cape St Vincent) with the four prizes and the disabled *Captain* in tow. At times other ships which had suffered damage to masts and rigging required assistance and, in the light winds, it was sometimes necessary to tow with ships' boats, a slow and laborious process. Jervis had no more than twelve ships fully ready for further action and some of these were involved in towing. It would have been unnecessarily foolhardy to have re-engaged the twenty-three Spanish ships still in sight.

It was on the cards that the Spaniards would restart the action; the two parts of their fleet – separated during the battle of the day before – were now combined, and in terms of relatively undamaged ships the odds were nearly two to one in their favour. Indeed, Córdoba may have had some such intention; several of the British ships' logs made reference to the Spanish fleet 'bearing down' from windward in the early afternoon of the 15th.

In practice it was not an easy thing to do. The Spanish ships, although apparently fit for action, had much damage to put right, and they were inexperienced in manoeuvring smartly as a fleet. The British would quickly have formed into a dangerous defensive formation, and twenty-two or -three Spanish ships, trying to overwhelm them, would have got in each other's way sufficiently to create total confusion. Córdoba decided to let bad enough alone and withdrew.

The Spaniards eventually found sanctuary in the port of Cadiz, which Jervis, with his fleet reinforced by subsequent arrivals from the Channel, settled down to blockade.

The battle had exposed the disastrous weakness of the Spanish navy, which was obviously a great satisfaction and comfort to the British, and it taught a number of other useful lessons. It was won by a fleet which had, in spite of setbacks, maintained the most effective station possible; it had demonstrated the value of audacity in attack, and it brought into prominence John Jervis, who now became Lord St Vincent.

The new earl, at 62 years of age, was a hard, tough man, who combined great interest in the health and welfare of his seamen with a stern and unyielding concept of discipline, applied as rigorously to officers as to the lower deck. St Vincent's fleet was no place for an idle, inadequate, or irresolute captain. As commander-in-chief in the Mediterranean, and later of the Channel Fleet, he was the source of a new spirit of determination and dedication which began to permeate the navy. When this was combined with the sort of enlightenment in leadership exemplified by men of the calibre of Nelson and Duncan, the navy began to move towards a new pinnacle of achievement.

The winter had exposed a number of shortcomings. Admiral Colpoys had failed to hold his station off Brest, and the Channel Fleet had failed to fulfil its purpose when a threat to Britain had been identified. Britain had lost the Mediterranean, partly at least because a senior officer had not absorbed the most basic of military principles – maintenance of the objective. An exceptional incidence of easterly gales had tested both sides and shown them, in some respects, wanting. However, the French, in the tenacity of their attempt on Ireland, had once again shown that, in spite of the limitations of their navy, it could never be disregarded. Jervis had fully demonstrated the value of determination in the face of unfavourable odds. The subsequent developments of the war at sea showed that the British navy was willing to learn.

CHAPTER 6

Camperdown

Of all the commands maintained by Britain in the closing years of the eighteenth century perhaps the least glamorous was the North Sea Fleet. Each of the other major stations had a cachet of its own: the West Indies brought prize money; the Mediterranean was, even then, romantic – there had been frequent action there and its climate was the best in which to serve on a ship equipped with few creature comforts; the Channel Fleet stood between England and the French and embodied the heart and soul of the navy. But the North Sea! Not only was the North Sea Fleet serving in waters which were often grim and cold but the enemy against whom it stood guard was Holland. Nobody felt much animosity against Holland; true, the Dutch navy was now hostile but only because it was an instrument of the French – France was the real enemy. Anybody watching out for the Dutch must have felt in something of a backwater confronted with a thankless task.

It was, in some ways, typical of the career of Vice-Admiral Adam Duncan that the command to which he was appointed in 1795 at the age of 66 should have been the North Sea Fleet. For he was an unflamboyant man, who had served the navy quietly and competently for fifty years; he had not done badly for prize money, and his appointment was not unconnected with the fact that his wife was the niece of the secretary of state for war. Had fate not brought him to Camperdown, he would have been just another admiral, promoted by seniority, appointed by influence and unknown to posterity. This would have been a pity because he was, in a quiet and undemonstrative way, an ideal commander of men. In looks like a rugby forward, human and humane, brave and steadfast, leading from the front, he saw his duty clearly and did it well as a matter of course. If Britain can look back with pride on the exceptional qualities and brilliance of Nelson, she can also consider with thankfulness that so often, when needed, there have been men like Duncan. In 1797, when the thoughts of St Vincent and Nelson were on wide oceans and distant harbours, Duncan's were on a familiar and mundane scene, the Texel.

Texel is the westernmost of the Friesian islands off the north coast of Holland, and what was referred to as the Texel was an area of comparatively deep water, inshore of the island of Texel, surrounded by sandbanks and shallows, but with a readily navigable outlet to the North Sea. In this natural harbour the Dutch had a fleet of about twenty-five ships, including ships of the line (only four of which were 74s), frigates and smaller vessels. When the French occupied Holland in the winter of 1794–5 this fleet was trapped in ice so thick that the French were able to capture it with cavalry and artillery. Although it was a military conquest, there was a sufficient body of republican opinion in Holland to make the occupation not entirely unwelcome, and the fleet remained manned by Dutchmen under a Dutch admiral, Jan Willem de Winter. The Dutch, whose very existence meant holding their own in constant warfare with the sea itself, were hardy and stubborn seafarers. More than a century earlier, they had, under Admirals van Tromp and de Ruyter, been very awesome opponents, stimulating the British to forge their navy into the formidable instrument in which they have taken pride ever since. The task of the North Sea Fleet was to keep the Dutch in the Texel; if they got out they would be a much greater menace than a French or Spanish force of similar size.

Yet the North Sea Fleet was the Cinderella of all the fleets kept by Britain to maintain her command of the sea. The best ships were sent to augment the fleets charged with watching the Spanish and the French. Neither were comparable, as seamen, to the Dutch but the Dutch had a handicap: not only was their fleet small but, in order to defend the shores of Holland, its ships had to be able to operate in shallow waters. In consequence the ships of the line in the Dutch fleet had been designed with shallow draught. For a sailing ship of given size and purpose there is an optimum draught. If the draught is to be subject to an arbitrary restriction, the performance of the ship will not be as good as it would have been if she had been designed with total freedom. The Dutch had a higher proportion of fourth-rates and 64-gun ships than other navies, and her 74s were likely to be more unhandy, and less seaworthy, than British 74s. It was considered reasonable therefore to equip the North Sea fleet with obsolescent 64-gun ships and old and tired 74s. Such ships would be unlikely to have the most dashing captains or the best crews. (Those seamen who volunteered, for example, would be more likely to volunteer for a smart ship, with a well-known captain and hopes of adventure and prize money.)

This was the fleet to which Adam Duncan was appointed in February 1795. It was a scratch fleet; it was small and, at times, was augmented by a number of Russian ships which could be considered only a liability. It was a frustrating situation for a man with high ideals of service who expected high standards from naval units in his command. Duncan was 66 and he was not short of money. He could have declined the appointment or resigned it when he saw its circumstances; no one would have greatly blamed him. But Duncan was no prima donna; instead of nurturing a sense of grievance at being given such unpromising material for so dreary a task, he recognised that there was a job to be done, and his nature was to see it done well.

For two years, Duncan and his unglamorous fleet watched the Texel like a cat watching a mousehole. It was a similar problem to that of blockading Brest, except that there was even less shelter in the easterly gales that could have released the blockaded fleet. Duncan realised, as John Jervis did, that the place for a blockading fleet was on the enemy's doorstep. Yet many of his ships were old and required frequent repairs in port. Even his own flagship, *Venerable*, was old and frail and was said to have an incurable leak which let rain into the admiral's cabin. It was a matter of constant compromise; as far as possible he kept his ships of the line at sea but out of sight from Texel, and his smaller ships close into the Dutch shore. He might often be obliged to allow ships to return to Yarmouth or the Thames estuary for repairs but the Dutch could never know how many. They were kept in constant apprehension of a menace just out of sight. This strategy, backed up by Duncan's dogged resolve to make the best possible use of the resources at his disposal, kept the Dutch in check from 1795 until the summer of 1797.

1797 was a year which dramatically displayed both the defects of the navy and its basic strength. It started with the failure of Bridport's Channel fleet to protect Ireland, or to catch a substantial French fleet at sea in British waters; it saw Jervis's victory at Cape St Vincent, the mutinies at Spithead and the Nore, and Duncan's victory at Camperdown. It was, though not apparent at the time, perhaps the most significant year of the whole period of the wars. It was not an obvious turning point after which everything went well – there were eighteen weary and often discouraging years to follow – but it was a period in which important lessons were taught and learned. The first embryonic concept of the importance of fair dealing for servicemen was impressed on the government; military leaders were given convincing demonstrations that victory follows wholehearted commitment and resolute refusal to be deterred by difficulties. Once these things were learned, the nation had taken the first steps on the long road to Trafalgar, Vitoria and Waterloo.

The mutiny at Spithead erupted in April and was settled by mid-May. Almost as the mollified crews of the Channel Fleet put once more out to sea, trouble broke out at the Nore. The Nore (named after sandbanks in the mouth of the Thames and meaning, in effect, the Thames estuary) was a separate command from Duncan's North Sea Fleet, which was based on Great Yarmouth. It was an administrative rather than a fighting organisation. Nevertheless, there was frequent contact between the two, and ships from the North Sea fleet frequently made use of the facilities at the Nore. There was a large element of perversity in the second mutiny. It broke out at a moment when, at Spithead, reconciliation was in the process of being completed. It continued long after the Channel Fleet had accepted the government's offers and was back at work. While at Spithead the leaders were democratically chosen delegates, at the Nore there emerged a 'president' who displayed inclinations toward self-importance. He seemed more interested in the processes of revolt than in achieving improvements in conditions for the men. Ships which were content to accept the agreements reached at Spithead found themselves coerced, by threat of bombardment, to join the mutineers.

Duncan, who respected his men and thought, correctly, that they respected him, could not believe that his ships, based at Yarmouth, would be affected. In this he was unduly optimistic and the discontent spread although, as at Spithead, there was very little violence and little action against individual officers. The first outbreak was on Duncan's flagship, *Venerable*, where on 30 April the crew refused duty. Duncan was outraged and at first had to be restrained from personally setting about the assembled rebels; persuaded to calm down, he listened to what they had to say. In fact, he did not need telling of the hardships of a seaman's life and was a principal advocate of reform; nevertheless he would have no truck with haggling over matters which, to him, were beyond discussion. His address to the men a few days later was a simple statement of duty and a reproof for their 'improper' conduct. Such were his manifest sincerity and the crew's innate good-heartedness that the written reply made to him on behalf of the crew is a model of an unservile but handsome apology. There was no more trouble on *Venerable*. A few days later there was an outbreak on *Adamant*, which Duncan also personally resolved by the force of his character and his fearless and straightforward methods. These two ships, *Venerable* and *Adamant*, remained loyal throughout the troubles that followed and were responsible for the fact that the tenuous thread by which Duncan held the Dutch under control never actually snapped.

On 26 May, the North Sea Fleet put to sea to resume the blockade, which had been dangerously weakened. Unfortunately, Duncan could not be on all his ships at once and four of them, out of the thirteen available, refused to sail. As the fleet approached the Dutch coast, seven more ships fell by the wayside one by one, their crews replacing the ensign with the red flag of rebellion and turning back to Yarmouth. Duncan was left with two ships, his flagship *Venerable* and *Adamant*. (His Russian contingent was not on the scene when wanted, either then or later at Camperdown.) His thoughts must have been bitter but, because his steadfastness and shining honesty of purpose had secured the loyalty of these two ships, and because it was in his nature to play his hand to the last card, he did not despair. *Venerable* and *Adamant* maintained the blockade alone, sailing inshore as close as they could and making signals, for the benefit of onlookers, to an imaginary fleet, which the Dutch could not be sure did not exist beyond the horizon. A fortnight later the mutiny at the Nore and Yarmouth, increasingly purposeless and with dwindling popular support, finally collapsed and Duncan was able to resume the blockade with his full fleet.

Beyond the North Sea the French were consolidating their recent acquisitions in northern Europe and, far to the south, General Napoleon Bonaparte was storming across northern Italy. In Brest the French fleet was recovering from its midwinter expedition to Ireland and repairing the ravages inflicted, not by the British but by the sea. There was little thought of or enthusiasm for any further adventures against the British Isles for the moment. In view of the state of the Channel Fleet, this was fortunate for Britain (although the mutineers had, throughout, maintained their willingness to return to duty if the

French should put to sea). However, in Wolfe Tone, the Irish rebel (or patriot, according to one's point of view), single-minded enthusiasm for an assault on Ireland still flourished undimmed and undiscouraged. He had been posted to the staff of General Daendels, the C-in-C of the Dutch army – possibly to get him out of the hair of the Directory in Paris – and his mind was active with schemes for furthering his great aim from within his new sphere of influence. News of the mutinies in the Royal Navy had been trickling through, so that Tone, not unreasonably, was convinced the time was ripe for a further attempt. The instrument with which to make it was to hand: the Dutch fleet and army were in good order and available. The good sense of his proposals was accepted by the French authorities and preparations were put in hand. Unfortunately for the French, there was an inevitable time-lag; it took time for the news of the mutinies and their extent to get through to Paris and, once approved, preparations for a combined operation inevitably took more time. Dutch troops embarked upon de Winter's ships in the Texel but long before everything was ready, the mutinies were over and the embarkation had been witnessed by Duncan's ships, once more fully on their station.

Nevertheless, it was still intended to go ahead with the operation. One can only sympathise with the Dutchmen packed into the ships. With the Channel and North Sea fleets alert, any expedition would have been foolhardy in the extreme and this must have been realised by the French authorities. Perhaps, although they would not have risked French troops in this manner, they were prepared to offer up Dutchmen as a sacrifice. However, it did not happen. This time the weather supported Britain and for nearly a month winds blew strongly from the west, completely foul for sailing from Holland down-Channel. Troops could only be kept crowded on shipboard, in packed and insanitary conditions, for a limited time and in mid-August 1797 they were disembarked. Things returned to normal, the Dutch cooped up in the Texel and Duncan's fleet waiting outside. Then, early in October, de Winter was ordered to sea. The orders were quite explicit: he was to take his fleet to sea and pick a fight with the British. There seems to be no good reason for this order. In the days when many decisions were made by inexpert revolutionary committees, it was not uncommon for ill-advised decisions to be made; perhaps it was thought that the North Sea Fleet could readily be beaten by de Winter, which would be good for public morale. It was a foolish order by any standards; at the very least it put at risk a perfectly good fleet which could be put to good use in some future, more important, operation. The order was made, however, and de Winter had to obey it.

After the North Sea mutiny ended, Duncan had taken his fleet for a long cruise to work it up to a proper state of seamanlike efficiency after the period of idleness and dissension. He was very conscious of the possibility, evidenced by the activity in the Texel, of an invasion attempt. By the beginning of October, the invasion scare seemed to have diminished, and many of his old ships were in need of dockyard attention. He therefore left two battleships and some smaller craft to watch the Texel and returned with the bulk of the fleet to Yarmouth for a short period. In the early morning of 9 October 1797 the lugger *Speculator* arrived with the news that the Dutch were at sea. The wind was north-westerly, fair for the Dutch coast, and the fleet put to sea at once.

The ships left to guard the Texel were six assorted vessels under the command of Captain Trollope of the 74-gun ship *Russell*. When the Dutch emerged on 7 October, Captain Trollope sent *Speculator* to warn Duncan, left the cutter *Active* on the spot to direct the fleet on its arrival, and with his remaining ships shadowed the Dutch, who had set off in a south-westerly direction. By the morning of 11 October, when Duncan and the fleet came up, de Winter, who had not travelled very far down the Dutch coast, had turned back towards the Texel. His orders were to fight but, although inexperienced as a naval commander, he knew Duncan's fleet was likely to be a very much tougher proposition than his committee masters had imagined. He wanted to fight in familiar shallow waters where he might contrive an advantage for his shallow-draught ships, and he wanted to be near the Texel to which stricken ships might retreat. De Winter was right to be cautious; not only was any suggestion that the mutinies might have affected the fighting ability of the British crews a fallacy, but he was out-gunned. Duncan's fleet of sixteen ships of the line not only had a slight preponderance of guns over de Winter's sixteen ships, but were equipped with carronades, which the Dutch did not have. Furthermore, good seamen though the Dutch were, they had not been at sea for at least two years and all their gun drill had been in harbour, whereas the British ships had been constantly exercised in gun drill at sea.

Duncan arrived off the Texel having learned from *Active* that the Dutch had gone south-west. He knew that, without troops aboard, they were unlikely to go far afield, and he was anxious that they should not slip back unscathed. He therefore turned in the direction from which the Dutch must come, should they return to the Texel. He made several casts inshore and out to sea to cover a wide track but the general direction of his progress was to the south-west. At 9 a.m. on 11 October, he came up with the ships under Captain Trollope, who was watching the Dutch and waiting.

As they sailed south-west in the path of the Dutch, the British fleet had become formed into two rough groups. One, under the command of Vice-Admiral Onslow, was ahead and further south (that is, to leeward); the other, under Duncan, was further north and to windward. The Dutch were heading roughly north-east, back to the Texel. It was not part of de Winter's plan to escape combat, merely to get himself in the most advantageous position, with shallow water immediately inshore of him. His ships were in line of battle and as the British approached, he waited for them, causing his ships to 'haul their wind', i.e. turn into the wind, stopping forward progress, and allowing themselves to be blown slowly towards the shoal water inshore.

It was a question of timing; if de Winter could entice the British to attack, so that when they got to close quarters the Dutch ships were over the shoals, then he would have won. The British ships would go aground, while the shallower Dutch ships would still have water to float in and could deal with each British ship at their convenience. But the timing was all-important. If he moved too obviously into the shallows before the British came up, the trap would be apparent and the British would hold off; if he left it too late, he would be caught by the British before he got into the safe shallow water. So the Dutch hauled their wind and waited.

Duncan's intention was to form a line of bearing before attacking (that is, his ships would attack in line abreast as Howe's had tried to do on the Glorious First of June); signals were made to put this plan into operation, and the first moves to carry out the necessary laborious forming-up were made. As he watched, realisation came to Duncan – it was taking too long. He looked at his ships, and saw that by the time they had got into line abreast and attacked the Dutch would have got just where de Winter wanted to be. Abandoning plans for a formal attack, Duncan flew the signals for each ship to pick its opponent, to attack at once and to pass inshore of the enemy's line to cut off their retreat to the shallows. He was relying on the fighting spirit

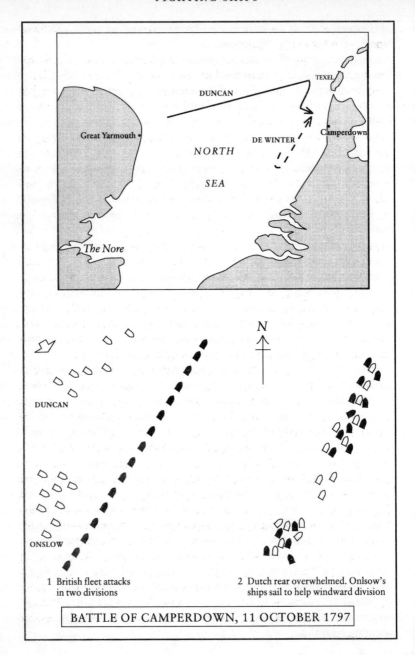

BATTLE OF CAMPERDOWN, 11 OCTOBER 1797

1 British fleet attacks
in two divisions

2 Dutch rear overwhelmed. Onslow's
ships sail to help windward division

of his captains and crews to go for the enemy without detailed direction, and he was not disappointed.

Onslow and his ships were nearer to the Dutch line than the windward group and they were the first into battle. There were eight of them and they set upon five of the enemy rear, which were quickly overwhelmed. This left help available for Duncan's division, which had attacked the forward part of the Dutch line. Among those in Onslow's division was *Director*, 64, whose captain was Bligh of *Bounty* fame. There are differing opinions of Bligh, and he no doubt had some defects as a commander. However, following the Nore mutiny, he is said to have interceded on behalf of his crew getting the number of men arrested substantially reduced, and he certainly did well at Camperdown. Once it was clear that the Dutch rear was being overwhelmed, on his own initiative Bligh made sail and pushed forward to the aid of Duncan's division, where he played a substantial part in the defeat of de Winter's flagship *Vrijheid*. This move, which was followed by *Powerful* and *Montagu*, was correct and proper because, for a while, the ships attacking the Dutch van by no means had everything their own way. Duncan's flagship, *Venerable*, was at one time assailed by at least three Dutch ships and could have been defeated; however, with the arrival from the rear of *Director*, *Powerful* and *Montagu* the situation was brought under control.

The action continued for two and a half hours and was hard and bloody. In all the sea battles of the period, it is noticeable that, when the attacker went in with vigour and determination, the casualties among his crews were usually very much lower than those of the defence. In this battle they were not so markedly different, an indication of the doggedness and resolution of the Dutch. The final result was decisive: seven Dutch ships of the line were taken, plus two fourth-rates and two frigates. The taking of the frigates was unusual, as it was normal practice for them to stand clear of battles between ships of the line. This, however, was one of the rare occasions when they fired upon unhandicapped battleships, a most courageous action since there could only be one result. One Dutch flag officer, Rear-Admiral Reyntjes, was killed and three including de Winter, were captured. De Winter was taken prisoner on board *Vrijheid* by Bligh's first lieutenant and put aboard *Venerable*; there he offered his sword in formal submission to Duncan, as was the custom, and Duncan said, 'I would rather take a brave man's hand than his sword' – which was typical of him.

The battle put an end to any question of the Dutch fleet exerting influence on further events; it did not put to sea again. Two years later the remains of it surrendered, without resistance, to a naval force supporting an abortive landing by British troops in Holland. Once again Duncan was commander-in-chief of the North Sea Fleet so the entire Dutch navy had been disposed of by naval forces under his command.

The nearest identifiable point to the scene of the battle on the flat, straight Dutch coast was the small village of Kamperduin and the anglicised form of this is the name by which it is known. That it became an almost forgotten battle is exemplified by the fact that Camperdown or Kamperduin is not even indicated on today's 10 km: 1 cm tourist maps. Nevertheless, it was of substantial, if not dramatic, significance. It eliminated for all time one threat to the vital trade between Britain and the Baltic, and it was achieved by steady attention to duty over a long period and determined courage at the moment when it was needed. It was a job well done and as such is a fitting memorial to Adam Duncan.

Rear-Admiral Horatio Nelson by Lemuel Francis Abbott
Nelson became Rear-Admiral and was invested as KB at the time of the battle of
Cape St Vincent in 1797. He became a Viscount after the battle of Copenhagen and
a Vice-Admiral in April 1801.

Victory, 1765
Under full sail including studding sails.

Nelson's flagships at anchor by Nicholas Pocock

On the far left is *Agamemnon*, Nelson's favourite command as a captain, broadside on is *Vanguard*, stern on is *Elephant*, on the right, stern on is *Victory*, beyond *Victory* is *Captain*.

The battle of cape St Vincent, 14 February 1797 by Robert Cleveley
Looking from the south during the final phase of the battle. The group in the centre includes *San José, San Nicolás* and *Captain* as Nelson formed his 'patent bridge'.

The battle of the Nile, 1 August 1798 by Matthew Nicolas Condy
At the moment of the destruction of *L'Orient* at 10pm.

The battle of Copenhagen, 2 April 1801 by Robert dodd
British ships moving up King's Deep to their battle stations, passing ships already in action.

H.M.S. VICTORY

		ARMAMENT – 1805	
Length of Gun Deck	186' 0"	Lower Deck	30 32-pounders
Length of Keel	151' 3"	Middle Deck	28 24-pounders
Moulded Breadth	50' 6"	Upper Deck	30 12-pounders
Extreme Breadth	51' 10"	Quarter Deck	12 12-pounders
Depth in Hold	21' 6"	Forecastle	2 68-pounders (Carronades)
Displacement (Approx)	3500 tons		
Burthen	2162 tons		

1. Poop Deck
2. Hammock Nettings
3. Mizzenmast
4. Quarter Deck
5. Ship's Wheel
6. Here Nelson fell
7. Pikes
8. Mainmast
9. Belfry
10. Fo'c'sle
11. Carronades
12. Foremast
13. Captain Hardy's Cabin
14. Upper Gun Deck
15. Nelson's Day Cabin
16. Nelson's Dining Cabin
17. Nelson's Sleeping Cabin with cot
18. Bowsprit
19. Middle Gun Deck
20. Wardroom
21. Tiller Head
22. Entry Port
23. Capstan
24. Galley and Stove
25. Low'r Gun Deck
26. Gun Room
27. Elm Tree Pump
28. Mooring Bits
29. Manger
30. Ork p
31. Dispensary
32. Aft Hanging Magazine
33. Lamp Room
34. Midshipman's Berth - here Nelson died
35. Forward Hanging Magazine
36. Powder Store
37. Powder Room
38. Aft Hold
39. Shot Locker
40. Bilge Pumps
41. Main Hold
42. Gunners Store
43. Main Magazine
44. Filling Room
45. Marines Walk
46. Admirals Barge
47. Ship's Launch
48. Light Room
49. Boarding Steps
50. 32lb Cannon
51. Bread Room
52. Spirit Room

Cut-away drawing of HMS *Victory*

Victory, a First Rate of 100 guns, was the largest Ship of the Line ever ordered for the Navy when the government commanded her construction in 1758. This drawing details her tremendous firepower and suggests the sheer size of Nelson's flagship.

Slung hammocks on the Lower Gundeck of HMS *Victory*
Giving some indication of the standard of comfort aboard a Ship of the Line.

CHAPTER 7

The Battle of the Nile

At about the same time as Adam Duncan was winning the battle of Camperdown, General Napoleon Bonaparte was imposing upon the Austrians the treaty of Campo Formio at the end of his successful North Italian campaign. For the time being Europe was pacified or bludgeoned into passivity and Napoleon was unemployed. The Directory in Paris was anxious to find him a fresh task before he began to think of political instead of military opportunities, and in October 1797 he was appointed commander-in-chief of the 'Army of England'. This army had not yet been assembled; but troops from Italy and northern Europe were available, and meanwhile the new C-in-C would have plenty to do in examining the Channel ports, and formulating a strategy for the invasion and subjection of the last enemy, Great Britain. It was now that the invasion of southern England began to seem, to the British, a serious possibility and the threat was to remain, in different degrees of urgency, for another eight years. It was not to be realised this time, however. Although there was only a weak army in England, Camperdown had made it clear that, in spite of the mutinies of 1797, the Royal Navy was as formidable as ever. Napoleon did not understand the sea, but he did understand that his troops could not cross the Channel in the face of the British navy; and he reported to the Directory accordingly. Instead, he and the veteran politician Talleyrand put forward the concept of striking at Egypt.

Attacking Egypt had a great deal to recommend it. Firstly, a successful operation would open up a land route to India, safe from the British navy, and Britain's trade with the East could be cut. Whether this would have been fatal to Britain or not, the French convinced themselves that it would. Secondly, it would bring increased territories and spheres of influence to France. Thirdly, it would occupy Napoleon far from Paris. Finally, it was practicable: the way was wide open, since the Mediterranean had been clear of the British for the last year. The Spaniards had been roundly defeated at Cape St Vincent, and John Jervis (now Lord St Vincent) had them bottled up in Cadiz, where he was keeping a tight blockade; but no attempt had been made to re-establish a British presence east of Gibraltar. The Directory was convinced, and Napoleon threw himself with his customary energy into preparations for the expedition; as well as troops, it was to include administrators, scientists, engineers, everybody and everything necessary for the establishment of a new French empire. Men, equipment and ships began to congregate in the vicinity of Toulon.

Meanwhile, in London, Prime Minister William Pitt the Younger was working hard on plans for breaking the deadlock in which Britain found herself. France was master in Europe; the British army available was far too small to have any hope of invading on its own, and Austria was exhausted and battered from her recent defeat. Unless permanent submission to France were to be accepted, something had to be done to initiate fresh resistance, in particular to encourage Austria to get up off the floor. Although it was already overstretched by the blockade, the one resource Britain had was her navy; it was physically possible for ships to be sent back into the Mediterranean. This was a course which would please the Austrians, and any success achieved might encourage them to take up the struggle again. News had been received of the activity around Toulon; its purpose was unknown but, if it involved a sea voyage, it would be vulnerable to the navy. Such an opportunity for effective action was not to be missed, even at the cost of weakening the fleets protecting Britain from possible invasion. Accordingly, on 2 May 1798, orders were sent to Lord St Vincent to detach part of his fleet and send it to the Mediterranean.

St Vincent, on his station off Cadiz, was the only British officer controlling any substantial force for hundreds of miles in any direction. Consequently, any information, from spies or well-disposed neutral observers, passed through his staff, and it was only he who could decide, on the basis of any report, whether to do anything, or to postpone action for at least a month by reporting it back to the Admiralty in London. Word of the activity at Toulon reached him at about the same time as it reached the cabinet. He was not afraid of responsibility and, without waiting for orders, he resolved at once to investigate. He had recently been rejoined by Rear-Admiral Sir Horatio Nelson, who had been at home recovering from the loss of his right arm, and St Vincent, who considered Nelson his most promising officer, had no hesitation in sending him with a small flotilla to find out what was happening. On 2 May 1798, the same day as the cabinet's order to St Vincent left London, Nelson hoisted his flag in the 74-gun *Vanguard* and, with two other battleships and four frigates, set sail for Toulon.

On 19 May, Napoleon left Toulon on his way to Egypt, accompanied by a huge fleet of merchant and troop ships, escorted by thirteen ships of the line and four frigates, under Admiral François Brueys. His route took him east along the Riviera coast to the north of Corsica, almost directly away from Nelson, who was in the Golfe du Lion, not much more than a day's sail behind. Had things gone well, Nelson must inevitably have caught up with the slow-moving convoy; and his frigates would have shadowed it while the news was sent back to St Vincent at Cadiz. Its systematic destruction would have been assured, and the subsequent history of Europe might have been very different. But things did not go well; they went very badly indeed. The north wind, the mistral, funnelling down the Rhone valley to the shallow waters of the Golfe du Lion, can whip up a vicious sea very quickly, and, with his mission on the point of accomplishment, just such a wind, extreme even for its kind, struck Nelson. His squadron was dispersed and his flagship suffered heavy damage to her masts. When the gale abated two days later, the crippled *Vanguard* was wallowing many miles south of Toulon, fortunately still in company with the other two ships of the line, *Orion* and *Alexander*. Captain Ball of *Alexander* saved the situation by towing *Vanguard* to a sheltered bay on the south coast of Sardinia, where she was able to anchor.

It is some measure of the navy's seamanship and resourcefulness that *Vanguard* was repaired and rerigged four days later. No amount of resourcefulness, however, could compensate for the second disaster that befell Nelson; not only did the gale prevent him from catching up with the French, but it deprived him of his frigates. They had seen the damage to the flagship at the onset of the gale, and then it was every ship for herself; when it was once more possible to look around and take stock, the battleships were far out of sight. *Vanguard* and her consorts might have gone anywhere, but, given the damage she had sustained, it was not unreasonable to suppose that, if she possibly could, she would have headed back to Gibraltar to make repairs. So back to Gibraltar the frigates went. Their loss was a serious blow to Nelson, beating back to Toulon with his three ships of the line. As has been seen, the function of frigates when attached to a fleet was reconnaissance. Fast and handy, they could range far and wide around the battleships, signalling back information which the admiral in command could obtain in no other way. Without them, the whole situation was changed.

While Nelson was coping with these difficulties, St Vincent, at Cadiz, had received orders from the Admiralty. They told him to send a strong detachment into the Mediterranean, to tackle the French 'armament' being prepared at Toulon and nearby ports. St Vincent had anticipated these orders, to a certain extent, by sending Nelson, with three battleships, on an armed reconnaissance; now he sent Captain Troubridge with ten 74s, one 50-gun ship, and the brig *Mutine* to join Nelson. *Mutine*, whose commander was Captain Thomas Hardy, an old friend of Nelson's, sailed at her best speed ahead of the main body of the fleet. On 2 June she encountered *Alcmene*, the senior of Nelson's frigates, *en route* back to Gibraltar; Hardy, of course, had no authority to change anything, but could only observe. When, therefore, *Mutine* came up to Nelson's ships three days later, Hardy was able to bring Nelson both good and bad news. The good news was that his first major command was on its way and, with it, his chance to achieve greatness; the bad news was that anything he did would have to be done without an essential part of any battle fleet.

When Troubridge arrived two days later in *Culloden*, the orders he brought were clear enough: 'I hereby authorise and require you,' St Vincent had written, 'to proceed . . . in quest of the Armament preparing by the enemy . . . On falling in with the said Armament, or any part thereof, you are to use your utmost endeavours to take, sink, burn or destroy it . . .'

'On falling in with' – there was the rub. First the enemy had to be found, and they could be anywhere on the wide ocean because, as Nelson discovered a few days later, they had left Toulon. Wherever they were, they had to be found without frigates. The long, dogged search began. The enemy could conceivably have sailed south of Sardinia and then west, possibly to make another attempt at Ireland, but Nelson thought this unlikely. St Vincent barred that way, and it would have been unlike the French deliberately to seek a battle which would, at the very least, endanger the success of whatever project they were engaged on. His first conclusion was that the object of the expedition was Sicily and that, as a preliminary, the French would first take Malta, then still under the control of the Knights of St John. He thought it might still be possible to catch them in some port on the way to Malta, and his fleet sailed down the west coast of Italy with *Mutine* investigating each anchorage as they passed. No trace was found, and Nelson arrived at Malta to find that it had indeed been taken by the French, but that they had left three days before, and clearly not for Sicily. On the approach to Malta, a sail had been seen, far to the east, which might easily have been the last of the French. If frigates had been available, they would have been sent to investigate; the French might have been caught at sea and, once again, the subsequent history of Europe would have been very different. But then, there are a lot of ifs in war. As Sicily was now ruled out, Nelson's next, and accurate, assessment was that the French destination was Alexandria; and to Alexandria he went.

Nelson was right about the destination of the French; what he could not have known, or guessed, was that they had not sailed there direct, but had gone via the south coast of Crete. The delay thus occasioned was sufficient to allow Nelson's fleet, which had taken the direct route, to arrive at Alexandria first. It was at once obvious that the French were not there and the British fleet sailed on. Still convinced that the French had designs on the Middle East, Nelson turned first north to the Turkish coast and then, finding nothing, back to Sicily.

Exasperating as the long, apparently fruitless, wanderings must have been to Nelson and his fleet, a great deal was being achieved. This was Nelson's first operation in charge of a substantial fleet, and he now had the opportunity to put into practice ideas that had long been germinating inside him. Previous battles had been fought with the admiral in charge making signals to his fleet, ordering, when necessary, the movements of individual ships as though they were pieces on a chess board. If signals were obscured by smoke or misunderstood, or if a ship were disabled at the wrong moment, then, to a greater or lesser extent, the admiral's plan was frustrated, and he had to improvise an alternative. By this time, a certain amount of confusion might have set in. It would have been better if the system of signals had enabled the admiral to explain, exactly and in detail, what he intended. Individual captains could then, when necessary, act on their own initiative but in general accordance with the plan.

Nelson's idea, revolutionary at the time, was to *tell* his captains what to do. To do this, he had to find opportunities to get his captains together, anticipate every possible combination of circumstances, and explain what he wanted them to do in each one of such combinations. Ideally he wanted his captains so attuned to his thinking that in any situation, foretold or not, they would automatically act in concert and as he would wish.

The long voyage through quiet summer waters provided many opportunities for captains to assemble on the flagship, and a new method of command was born. In the great cabin of *Vanguard*, tactics to be employed in a wide range of circumstances were examined; different situations in which they might encounter the French were imagined; and Nelson's wishes in each of them made known. The waste and futility of indecisive battles was emphasised. The object was not just to take a few French ships, but to clear the French fleet from the sea, so that the situation in the Mediterranean would be completely altered.

Nelson's heartfelt conviction, and his flair for imparting communal purpose, gave each captain two invaluable gifts, first, a clear knowledge of his duty in any situation, and, second, the *esprit de corps* which comes from being part of an efficient organisation, whose members are also friends. Nelson's 'band of brothers' was being formed and they became, as near as may be, unbeatable. Frustration must have been intense as the fleet turned back again to Sicily, but the period of waiting was nearly over.

While Nelson was on his way back to Sicily via the Turkish coast, having left Egypt behind him, the French arrived at Alexandria, and the invasion was under way. While they rapidly established themselves as masters of Egypt, Nelson revictualled his fleet in the harbour of Syracuse on the east coast of Sicily. Then, still convinced that the French were somewhere in the Levant, he turned east again for Cyprus via the coast of Greece. On 28 July, the fleet was off the island of Sapientzo, the most south-westerly of the Greek islands, and *Culloden* under Captain Thomas Troubridge entered the port of Koroni, on the mainland nearby. Greece was then under Turkish control. The Turks were better disposed to Britain than to France, and they gave Troubridge the information the fleet had been waiting for since the end of May: the French had gone to Alexandria. With *Culloden* towing a small French brig laden with wine, which she had captured off Koroni, the fleet turned south-east for Egypt.

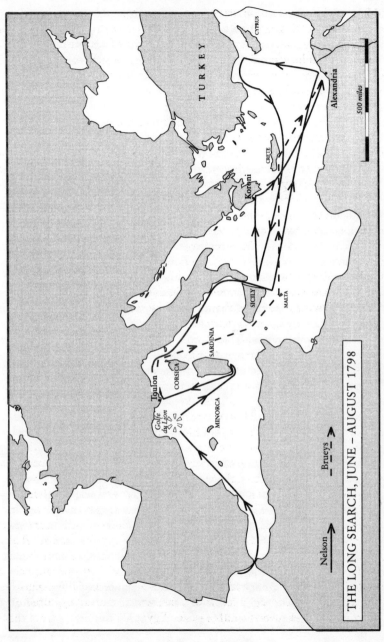

CYPRUS

TURKEY

Alexandria

500 miles

CRETE

Koroni

SICILY

MALTA

SARDINIA

Toulon

CORSICA

Golfe
du Lyon

MINORCA

Brueys ▬▬▶

Nelson ▬▬▶

THE LONG SEARCH, JUNE – AUGUST 1798

On the 1 August 1798, the coast of Egypt appeared on the horizon to the south-east; the day was fine, a moderate breeze blew from the NNW and *Alexander* and *Swiftsure* were scouting well ahead, on the starboard bow of the main body of the fleet. Shortly after midday, *Alexander* signalled the presence of French ships in Alexandria harbour. It was soon established that these were the merchant ships, which made it a near certainty that the warships would be close at hand, the most obvious place being Aboukir Bay, about ten miles along the coast to the east. *Alexander* and *Swiftsure* were recalled, and the fleet turned to larboard towards the town of Aboukir, on its low-lying spit of land, beyond which lay Aboukir Bay and the mouths of the Nile. At about half past two, *Zealous*, whose captain, Samuel Hood, had kept her up to the east in the hope of just such an event, signalled that sixteen enemy ships were at anchor in Aboukir Bay. The long chase was over; by early evening the fleet was poised off Aboukir, ready for the final act.

From the spit of land at the western end of Aboukir Bay a reef runs out to sea, in a north-easterly direction, for about four miles. On its seaward side there is, in general, comparatively deep water close in; on its inshore or bay side, there is a large area of water about four fathoms (24 feet) deep, with many sandbanks over which the depth is two fathoms or less. The French fleet was anchored in a line, with a slight dogleg in it, roughly NW–SE and NNW–SSE along the edge of the four-fathom area, the head of the line being close in to the end of the reef. On the reef is a small island, still known as Nelson's Island, on which the French had mounted a number of guns; these were of small calibre and, in the event, of little importance. The four French frigates were anchored inshore of the French line.

In fire power the French had a slight theoretical advantage over the British, in that their ships included *L'Orient* of 120 guns, three 80-gun ships and nine 74s against Nelson's thirteen 74s and one 50. In practice, however, they stood little chance. For the reasons mentioned in Chapter 1, one sees a curious inconsistency in French naval performance. Their fleet had performed its duty adequately in 1794; in 1796 it had, despite its lack of training, displayed great determination and courage in its attempt on Ireland. Whenever battle was joined, they fought with courage and tenacity against a much more skilful enemy. But it seemed as though action had to be forced upon them before their energy became released. There was a legacy of caution from the long period in which France, primarily a land power, regarded her navy as a secondary adjunct to her army, not expected to achieve great things on its own. Her great admirals in the past had risen above this thinking, but those of the revolutionary period had little inducement to do so; emphasis had been on keeping her warships intact, a Maginot Line mentality had developed, and imaginative enterprise received little encouragement.

All this must be part of the reason why Admiral Brueys had chosen such a totally defensive position. He relied, mistakenly, on the shallows to protect his inshore side but, even had this tactic been effective in practice, his position was one from which he could not win. At the very best he might have so battered the British fleet that it withdrew, but after withdrawing it could have repaired its damage and come again. The French could not withdraw, at least not in the presence of an enemy; any move from their anchorage must have broken up their formation, turning it into a collection of individual ships which could be destroyed one by one. Even their frigates were all at anchor, instead of patrolling offshore to bring warning of any hostile fleet. The picture of the ships, anchored where they were, calls to mind small, frightened, animals huddling together, as far into a hole as they can get, in fear of some predator. It was nearly dusk when the British fleet came in from the sea, sails red in the setting sun; perhaps, on the French ships, the watching crews really did feel in a strong position, but it seems more likely that there were some sickening last-minute doubts.

Nelson, about five miles north of Aboukir, ordered his fleet to heave to and prepare to anchor by the stern. Then came the signal that the enemy's van and centre were to be attacked; this signal, which was confirmation of methods long since worked out in *Vanguard*'s great cabin, defined precisely how the battle was to be fought, and each captain fully understood what it meant. The French were anchored more or less in line with the wind, which was from the NNW and moderate, their van being to windward and their rear to leeward. Nelson's signal meant that the whole of the attack by his fourteen ships was to be concentrated on the first six or seven ships in the French line. The ships in the rear of the line would see that the attack was being concentrated on the ships ahead of them, but would be able to do very little about it. If a ship in the rear weighed anchor, it would first drift further downwind until the sails began to take effect and drive the ship forward; then it would be unable to sail directly towards the van, which would be dead to windward. It would have to sail, on the larboard tack, almost at right angles to the direction of the van, until it was far enough away to come about and sail back towards the battle. If everything had been done correctly, it would then be able to turn into the wind and attack one of the ships assailing the van or centre. All this would take time, and there would be a good chance that the ships first attacked would be overwhelmed before help arrived.

The pattern of the battle having been conveyed to the captains by this one order, further signals were flown, to turn to starboard, to let the sails draw and to engage the enemy; in effect, 'Go'. There were no other signals, except the standard one, always flown in battle, 'Engage the enemy more closely.'

The British ships turned, and in the order in which they were lying ran down towards Aboukir Bay. The first ship to round the end of the reef and get into action was *Goliath*. Its captain, Thomas Foley, decided to take the inshore side of the French line, between the ships and the sandbanks. This was not a daring chance, taken in the heat of the moment, but a carefully thought-out decision, made by a professional in accordance with principles already defined in meetings on board *Vanguard*. The French ships were anchored by the bow only, which meant that when the wind changed they would swing round to point into it (there is no tide in the Mediterranean). They lay roughly parallel to the shore, so when the wind became more easterly, their sterns would swing round to lie towards the shore. To do this, there must have been enough water inshore of their present position for a ship to float. It seems a fairly obvious deduction, and perhaps it was to a seaman, but the French apparently did not expect it to be made. One report suggested the French were so sure they would not be attacked on the inshore side that they left the larboard side of their decks cluttered with stores and the gunports unopened. This must have been a lapse of memory on the part of its author; clearing ship for action was a drill, and there is no reason why the officers should vary a drill in order to leave material – probably combustible – on a gundeck, even if they did think they were safe on one side. Certainly, the logs of the British ships do not suggest any particular delay in the French larboard guns opening fire.

If Admiral Brueys believed he could not be attacked on the inshore side, one can only sympathise with his horror as, at the outset of the attack, he had to face the appalling fact that this defence had failed.

Throughout the next ninety minutes, as darkness fell, the attacking ships came in, each arrival brutally emphasising the fact that not only had he overlooked a deadly danger, but he was not going to be given the chance to make anything like an even fight of it. Of the thirteen ships coming in, seven came down the inshore side of his line and six down the seaward side; none went further than his flagship, *L'Orient*, which was halfway down the line. In other words, his first seven ships were to be bombarded by thirteen, and there was very little the six ships behind him could do about it.

It was thirteen ships and not fourteen because *Culloden*, in her haste to get into battle, had fouled the end of the reef off Aboukir and stuck there. The precise point is still marked Culloden Reef on today's charts. It was a shocking anticlimax, at a moment when everybody was keyed up to a pitch of maximum excitement and anticipation, but there was nothing to be done. She did not get off until the following day when other ships could spare time to help her.

Neither *Culloden*'s accident nor anything else could help Admiral Brueys. The first seven ships in the French line were doomed and it looked as if nothing could stop the eventual destruction of the remaining six. None of them had weighed anchor in an attempt to get into the fight; it would have been a difficult operation because, by the time it was apparent that the van and centre were to be taken out first, it was dark. Nevertheless, there was clear water, free of shallows, to seaward of the line and, although it would have been a pretty desperate enterprise, a determined captain would have tried it. Again, there is the contrast between the hypnotised inaction of the ships in the rear, and the desperate courage of the Frenchmen in the van, who fought without hope till they could fight no more. The first ship in the line was *Le Guerrier*, which was engaged on her inshore side only by *Zealous*. Captain Hood recorded in a letter to his uncle that *Le Guerrier* fought for three hours until she had only one gun left which would fire and still she would not strike; finally, Hood sent an officer across in a boat, and he managed to persuade her officers to strike and call a halt to the slaughter. Most of the ships fought for an hour and a half or more, even with British ships on either side of them. Brueys, badly wounded in both legs, had himself placed in a chair so that he could remain on his quarterdeck, where he was eventually killed. The captain of *Tonnant*, in similar circumstances, had himself braced upright in a tub.

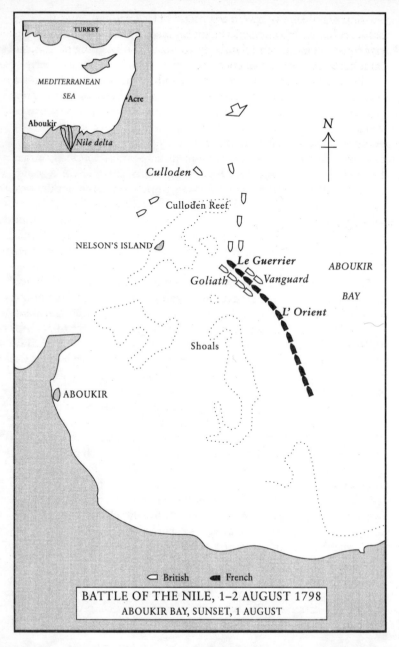

TURKEY

MEDITERRANEAN
SEA

Acre

Aboukir

Nile delta

N

Culloden

Culloden Reef

NELSON'S ISLAND

Le Guerrier

ABOUKIR

Goliath *Vanguard*

BAY

L' Orient

Shoals

ABOUKIR

◁ British   ◀ French

BATTLE OF THE NILE, 1–2 AUGUST 1798
ABOUKIR BAY, SUNSET, 1 AUGUST

Admiral Villeneuve was in command of the rear and, long after the battle, came in for some criticism for his inaction. He defended himself vigorously: it occurred to nobody to go to the help of the van, he said, because it was impracticable.

The matter of support from the rear became academic at about 9.30 p.m. when, with the resistance of the first seven ships fading, *L'Orient* caught fire. Fire was the most deadly danger to wooden warships and, unless it could be smothered very quickly, was invariably followed by an explosion. The British ships with which *L'Orient* was engaged and the French ships anchored behind her began to weigh their anchors and drift away from her. No other danger was so great as being close to a first-rate, with perhaps 15 tons of gunpowder in her magazine, about to blow up. The explosion when it came must have been one of the biggest the world had seen and it brought the battle temporarily to a halt. For a while there was silence, broken only by the splashing of falling debris, which seemed to go on for an impossibly long time. There followed a sort of stunned lull. Except for an occasional report, the guns were silent; there was the sound of axes clearing fallen rigging, an occasional shout or splash, and the sounds of boats picking up survivors of *L'Orient*. Captain Miller, on *Theseus*, tried to stifle his feelings of pity by thinking of atrocities the French were said to have committed, but he felt constrained to try to stop his crew cheering; he had no use for the French, but it didn't seem decent to cheer at such a cataclysmic loss of life.

Now, men who had worked and fought for twelve hours or more suddenly became aware of how tired they were. Anyone whose work allowed him to ease up for a moment flopped where he stood and surrendered to sleep. Officers tried to force their tired minds on to the next job to be done. Nelson had been wounded and taken below, concussed and apparently blinded, but at that moment no amount of orders from the flagship would have made much difference. What mattered then was how many men there were with the dedication and willpower to force themselves to think of the next stage. They had been totally engrossed in a battle which had stopped; now what they had to do was to restart it in new circumstances, requiring different methods.

The situation was altered. When the battle started, there had been a line of French ships, anchored close to the shallows but clearly indicating a navigable stretch of water. The task of the British had been to knock out the first six or seven enemy ships, and then to weigh anchor and sail slowly along the line to destroy the rear. Now there was no line; the ships near *L'Orient* had weighed anchor and drifted astern; they formed a group, perhaps a mile downwind, clearly visible in the light of the rising moon, in which desultory shots were exchanged as guns could be brought to bear. To reach that group a ship would have to sail across a stretch of open water, without any indication of where the sandbanks were. Not only that but most of the British ships, although victorious, had suffered damage to their rigging, and would not be properly controllable until temporary repairs and clearance of wreckage had been carried out. However, Nelson's training was bearing fruit; without orders from the flagship, the captains were grappling with the problem. Captain Miller on *Theseus* sent a warrant officer in a boat to take soundings and then, as there was nothing else he could do for the moment, fell asleep. He was woken by Captain Hood of *Zealous*, who had come to see if some concerted action could be worked out. Miller was able to tell him that he was working on it. Before the boat taking soundings had returned to *Theseus*, a boat from the flagship had arrived; Nelson, whose wound was less serious than at first supposed, had returned to his quarterdeck and had sent messages, ordering support for the two ships which were still in sporadic action against the French in the group downwind. Miller and Hood were already doing all that could be done. As soon as the information about the depth of water came back, *Theseus* weighed anchor and ran down to the leeward ships, but by the time she got there firing had, for the moment, stopped. Nothing was spoiling so Miller decided to wait until more ships came down to join him, so that there would be overwhelming force against the remaining French ships.

With men on both sides stupid with fatigue, the damage to the ships, the darkness, and the uncertainty about the depth of water, everything that happened that night, in the small hours of 2 August, happened very slowly. Dawn was about to break before anything like concerted action restarted. Now several British ships were moving downwind to assist *Alexander*, *Majestic* and *Theseus* to restart the battle against the remaining six of the French; as they did so the 80-gun *Guillaume Tell* and *Généreux*, 74, weighed anchor, not to sail into battle but to leave the scene. In doing this, Villeneuve, who was in *Guillaume Tell*, was perfectly correct; he had no hope of affecting the issue of the battle and it was his duty to save what ships he could. All the same, it was a humiliating duty: if Villeneuve did in truth commit suicide after Trafalgar, it could well be that depression, fed by the unheroic roles it seemed to be his lot to play throughout his career, contributed to his despair. Both ships and two frigates got away; they had too great a start for the British ships, most of whom had received some damage to sails and rigging. *Zealous* got near enough to exchange one broadside but she was recalled, because she could not have stopped them on her own. In the event, both *Guillaume Tell* and *Généreux* were taken in the following months.

Of the remaining four French ships, two ran aground and surrendered; *Timoléon* ran aground under fire from *Theseus* but refused to surrender, and *Tonnant*, completely dismasted but defiant, stayed at her anchorage and also refused to surrender. The British held off; neither ship was going anywhere and there was no point in further slaughter. The following day, 3 August 1798, *Timoléon*'s crew set her on fire and *Tonnant* finally surrendered.

The task of the 'band of brothers' had been thoroughly finished; it was the most complete naval victory in history. Napoleon's link with France had been cut and the British were back in the Mediterranean. The Egyptian expedition soon came to a halt and thereafter things began to look a little bit brighter for Britain.

Admiral Brueys had asked for defeat by tying up his ships in such a dangerous and inflexible position; on the other hand, Nelson and his fleet, given the opportunity, had responded to it with total professionalism. Nelson did not change everything in a flash, but his method of treating his subordinates as members of a team, rather than pieces to be moved about a board, had been thoroughly justified. Good and gifted commanders had always instinctively created among their men a sense of being part of a brotherhood, rather than merely the recipients of orders; Nelson's deliberate cultivation of this method was an early step towards recognition of it in high places. Two hundred years later, Nelson's way is the basis of all training of military leaders.

Above all, the battle demonstrated the great significance of sea power. Napoleon's army was not destroyed at once; he made a desperate attempt to reach Asia Minor, where he could have found most of his needs, but he was stopped at Acre by the Turks, who were supported by Sir Sidney Smith. Cut off by Nelson from French supplies, he could make no further attempt and the French army stagnated in Egypt until beaten by General Sir Ralph Abercromby in

1801. By the proper use of sea power, Britain, with fourteen ships and about 7,000 men, had brought to a halt the most powerful army the world had yet seen.

CHAPTER 8

Copenhagen

The battle of Copenhagen was a tragic one in that it was fought between people who were not really enemies and it turned out, too late, that it was unnecessary. This is not to say that it could have been foreseen as unnecessary; the reason for embarking on the course which led to it was as compelling as any reason could be – to protect England from invasion.

Invasion of England had been an aim of the French government since 1797. At that time it was shelved in favour of the expedition to Egypt but a second attempt to land troops in Ireland was made. By now the British had a lively awareness that 'Boney' might come to England. Although it was not until some five years later that Napoleon put in hand preparations for a large-scale invasion, it was clear to all that an attempt would have to be made sometime if he hoped for final victory, and such an attempt might have been in preparation at any time. In 1801 it was considered that the threat was increasing; events in Egypt were at a standstill, Napoleon himself was finishing off the Austrians in Central Europe, and it seemed quite on the cards that the next move would be against England.

In fact, although delayed by the Treaty of Amiens, it was the next military enterprise to which Napoleon turned his mind; he could well have tried it in 1801. Britain's only real defence, in 1801 as in 1804–5, was to keep the French navy pinned down. So long as Napoleon could not mass his ships, his troops could not cross the Channel. Blockade of the French ports, from being something of a part-time occupation, had become of first importance.

Lord St Vincent was now in command of the Channel Fleet, and the old days of gentle blockading by a fleet based on Spithead were gone; the fleet's station was now off Brest, and there it was required to stay and endure, whatever the weather. It was a hard service for ships as well as men, and called for constant supplies of fir for spars, hemp for rope and flax for sails. Stop these items and the blockade would come to an end; with no blockade, invasion would be a near certainty. Now there had developed a very real threat to these supplies. Instigated by France and supported by the Russian Tsar Paul I, Prussia and Denmark were about to join with Russia and Sweden in a treaty of armed neutrality, the chief effect of which would be to close the Baltic to British trade. Since the principal supplies Britain got from the Baltic states were precisely those on which its navy depended – fir for spars, hemp for rope and flax for sails – Britain had no alternative. The treaty of armed neutrality had to be stopped at all costs.

Denmark was the key to the situation as far as the British government was concerned; Denmark had an effective navy and she could control the narrow waters which form the entrance to the Baltic. The Danes did not want to be involved but they were vulnerable to their powerful neighbour, Russia. If Russia wanted Denmark to sign the treaty, the Danes had little alternative. A special envoy was sent by Britain to the Crown Prince of Denmark (who held effective power) in an attempt to persuade him otherwise, but without great hope of success. It was felt that more powerful arguments were necessary to reinforce diplomacy and to take over if and when diplomacy failed.

Accordingly, a fleet was to be sent to the Baltic. The presence of a substantial force off Copenhagen might convince the Danes that they had more to fear from the British navy than from Russia; then the negotiations might develop satisfactorily for Britain. Failing that, the Danish fleet must be destroyed. Subsequently, and as a secondary objective, similar pressure was to be put on Russia. It was not a mission which aroused any enthusiasm in Britain or in the navy. Denmark had done no direct harm to Britain and the proposed treaty was, though a real enough threat, not a very dramatic *casus belli*. Like the destruction of the French fleet in Oran after France's collapse in 1940, it was regarded as a distasteful job which had to be done.

The obvious commander for such an expedition was Nelson: his victory at the Nile had fully demonstrated his ability, and he was available, having recently been appointed second in command to St Vincent in the Channel Fleet. Unfortunately, he was still a fairly junior vice-admiral and there were other, more senior, men who could be employed. Besides, the gloss of his reputation had been a little dulled by recent immature behaviour. He had returned from the Mediterranean a few months before, not in a frigate as a modest hero should, but via a tasteless and tinselly progress through the capitals of unoccupied Europe in the company of Sir William and Lady Hamilton. It was an unhappy period in Nelson's career, and for a time the least estimable part of his character seemed to be in the ascendant. Nevertheless, no one could doubt that he was the best fighting admiral the navy had, and it was obvious that he ought to be employed. The problem was solved by appointing him second in command to Sir Hyde Parker. Sir Hyde was over sixty and had no recent fighting experience. He had been an adequate captain but his experience as an admiral had been as C-in-C of the West Indies station, an excellent post for prize money, but not for experience of controlling a fleet. However, he had administrative ability so the Admiralty was covered both ways: if diplomacy won the day, Hyde Parker could cope; if it did not, there was Nelson.

The fleet which assembled at Great Yarmouth in March 1801 consisted of two second-rates, *London*, which was Hyde Parker's flagship, and *St George*, which was Nelson's, fifteen third-rates, two fourth-rates, four frigates and a number of smaller craft. The atmosphere in which preparations took place was far from happy. Nelson was clearly disgruntled with Parker and Sir Hyde was suspicious of Nelson. Parker, as later events were to show, was slow to take decisions and lacked a sense of urgency in implementing them once taken. Furthermore, he had just married a young wife and, perhaps understandably, was in no hurry to exchange her company for the cold, grey waters of the Baltic. Nelson was anxious to be off, partly because to leave as soon as possible was the right thing to do. The greater the delay, the greater the chance of the coming spring melting the winter ice in the northern Baltic ports, thus enabling the Russians to link up with the Danes. The standard of the Russian navy was not high but, added to the Danish fleet, it would have made the odds distinctly unfavourable.

There was a further reason to hurry, well understood by Nelson, although not emphasised in Parker's orders from the Admiralty and certainly not appreciated by him. It was intended to use strong-arm tactics; regrettable as this might be, there was no point in half measures. If the fleet arrived off Copenhagen while the talks with the government's special envoy were in progress, it would be a much more effective gesture than a fleet known to be on its way but not yet in sight. Further, its presence would strengthen the hand of those Danes who, though caught up in power politics, were not pro-French. It would have been possible to tell Napoleon that, with a bellicose fleet on their doorstep, they had no alternative but to give in to the British. Delay would not only give the Danes more time to prepare for battle, but would also mean that any chance of the fleet's presence preventing a battle would be thrown away.

Nelson was unable to bring any personal influence to bear to hurry Parker. Eventually, Lord St Vincent, who had just become First Lord of the Admiralty, sent a private letter to Sir Hyde, strongly hinting that, if he knew what was good for him, he would get to sea at once. Sir Hyde, who had planned to wait at least until the following weekend, when his wife was giving a ball, took the hint and gave orders to sail. The fleet left Yarmouth on the morning of Thursday, 12 March.

On the voyage to Denmark, Parker began to display signs of excessive caution. The wind was fair; a reasonable estimate of the time to reach Danish waters would have been four or five days. It took a week, mainly because of over-caution in approaching the Danish coast. It was not until 19 March that the fleet anchored off Vinga (anglicised in the ships' logs to 'Wingoe') on the Swedish shore, about 200 miles north of Copenhagen.

If the fleet had pressed on, it could have been off Copenhagen before the talks there were finished. Parker's orders required him to give the Danish Government forty-eight hours' notice of opening any hostilities; this could have been done with the fleet anchored in sight of the city, and, as suggested above, it just might have resulted in an agreement with the Danes. If, as was perhaps more likely, they had still decided to fight, they would have had only forty-eight hours to prepare. Parker, however, stayed at Vinga and sent the ultimatum from there. This was bad for two reasons: first, any possible moral effect of the close presence of the fleet was lost; second, the frigate bearing the message took three days to get to Copenhagen and back, to which would have to be added at least two days for the fleet to get into action. So the Danes were given at least five days' warning instead of two; in the event the delay was considerably longer.

The story of the preliminaries to the battle of Copenhagen reads like an indictment of Sir Hyde Parker. Yet he was in an almost impossible position; it was quite clear that his superiors – the government –

would greatly prefer a solution which did not involve hostilities with the Danes, and Sir Hyde was in the hot seat. Any step he took might be the one which changed the situation from one in which a peaceful solution was just possible to one in which warfare was inevitable. A man with the right sort of imagination and flair might have seen clearly what he should do, a lesser man might well have been over-whelmed with the need for careful consideration of every step before it was taken. Nelson had the right sort of flair but Parker did not; he was like a man in a minefield wondering where to put his foot. We, who could have done no better, should sympathise with Parker when the frigate *Blanche* returned, bringing a dusty answer from the Danes. Now a definite move would have to be made.

Copenhagen is on the east coast of the island of Zealand (Sjælland), which almost plugs the entrance to the Baltic between Sweden and the Danish mainland. There are two ways by which the town can be reached from the Kattegat (the sea north of Zealand). The long way involves sailing round Zealand, passing through the channel known as the Belt between Zealand and the Danish mainland, and approaching from the south; the short way is via the channel known as the Sound between Zealand and Sweden. Sir Hyde moved the fleet to a headland called Kullen, or the Koll, about 100 miles nearer to the Sound but he felt considerable anxiety about entering it. The navigable channel was narrow and shallow and its entrance was guarded by a substantial gun installation – the fortress of Kronborg at Helsingør (Elsinore, of *Hamlet* fame) about 25 miles north of Copenhagen. At close range, shore-based batteries were a great danger to wooden ships, they were unsinkable and could fire red-hot shot. Sir Hyde was right to be concerned about Kronborg but there was an answer. The range of the guns was limited and it was possible to pass Kronborg close to the Swedish shore and out of range; if the Swedes did actively support Denmark, which was unlikely at this stage, their batteries were not very powerful and no great threat. The alternative was to go round via the Belt which could easily take a week.

To try to resolve his uncertainties Sir Hyde called a meeting on his flagship. It was attended by Nelson and the men who had been at the abortive talks in Copenhagen, William Drummond, the erstwhile ambassador, and Nicholas Vansittart, the special envoy. It was not attended by Captain Otway, Parker's flag captain (that is, the captain of the flagship), Captain Dommett, the captain of the fleet (Parker's senior staff officer) or Captain Tomlinson who, as an acknowledged

Baltic expert was aboard the flagship, *London*, as a volunteer.

That two civilians should be involved in what was a purely military decision was unusual. Drummond might be expected to have picked up some knowledge of the Danish defences but it could be only inexpert knowledge. He had not the experience to form an accurate appraisal of the calibre of the coastal artillery or of its power. However, a conclusion was reached and it was decided that the fleet should take the long route via the Belt. Having reached the southern end of the Sound the action to be taken would be governed by the wind. Were it favourable, an assault on the Danish fleet at Copenhagen would be made from the south; if not the fleet would sail east and north to try the possibilities of an attack on Russia. It seems uncharacteristic of Nelson that he should be associated with postponement of action and general uncertainty; but he had reached a stage at which he felt any decision was better than none at all. Also, he thought the first objective of the expedition should have been Russia rather than Denmark. So this development, although resulting from a style of command very different from his own, was not displeasing to him. Parker gave his orders and at 4.00 p.m. on 24 March the fleet weighed anchor and sailed south-west.

Captains Otway and Dommett had not been consulted, and it was only from the direction in which the fleet was heading that they realised that the intention was to go via the Belt. Having some knowledge of the channels and winds in those waters, they were appalled at the complications which, they believed, could arise; they sought an interview with Parker and begged him to reconsider. Poor Sir Hyde, having acted on advice rather than his own conviction, now found himself with different advice which seemed equally compelling. Once again the fleet anchored and Nelson was called from *St George* for further discussion. This time a firm plan was finally settled upon, under which the Danish fleet would be attacked via the Sound and Nelson would lead the assault. No sooner had the die been cast than the wind turned SSW – foul for the Sound – and the fleet had to remain at anchor.

This delay was not unproductive. Nelson, at last, had clear instructions and had in his mind the general lines on which he would attack. The wait for a fair wind enabled him to do as he had done on the way to the Nile; the captains under his command were brought aboard his flagship and the process of attuning them to his intentions and methods began.

The wind became fair for the Sound on 28 March but once again there was delay. Parker decided to send a message to the Danish commander of Kronborg Castle to ask him whether he had orders to open fire, should the British fleet enter the Sound. Sir Hyde was still hoping against hope that some miracle would bring about the desired result, without his having to take the fateful step that would set the Baltic ablaze and for which he might later be held culpable.

No miracle occurred. The Danish commander, very sensibly, sent back a reply which was non-committal and clearly only a delaying tactic. Parker could put off the evil day no longer, for the reply amounted to a declaration of war. The fleet was ordered to move but by now the wind was foul again, and it could move only a short way before anchoring slightly nearer the entrance to the Sound. However, on the following day, Monday, 30 March, the wind veered again to the north west; at 6.30 a.m. the fleet weighed anchor and moved into the Sound and towards Copenhagen.

While all the moves and hesitations of the last ten days had been going on in the Kattegat, the Danes had been preparing their defences. These consisted of a line of warships, armed hulks and large rafts fitted with guns to form floating batteries. This line extended the whole length of Copenhagen waterfront and was augmented by three land-based batteries or forts. The most powerful and permanent of these, which is still standing, was the Trekroner Fort at the north end of the line near the channel which leads to the inner harbour. In front of Copenhagen the Sound, running roughly north and south, divides into two navigable channels with shallows either side and a third, central shallow area between. The channel nearer to the town is known as the Kongedybet, or King's Deep, the central area of shallows is called the Middle Ground and the far, or more easterly, channel is the Holland Deep. The Danish floating defences were moored in front of the town along the western edge of the King's Deep; to attack them it would be necessary to navigate this channel, which is little more than a quarter of a mile wide with mud banks on either side. All navigational aids had been removed.

To man these defences, which had been made ready with great ingenuity and energy, many more men were needed than the small Danish navy could provide, and volunteers were required. The Danes were then, as now, a quiet, orderly, unmilitaristic people, but they set about defending their homes in a manner which was no less determined for being quiet and orderly. Proclamations were posted in the king's name ordering 'Our dear and true Danish landsmen immediately to prepare themselves to arms in readiness to report at times and in places that councillors will make known'. This they did, and a stream of steady, respectable householders and tradesmen assembled to make good shortages of men on ships and to man the floating batteries. In a letter to Emma Hamilton, Nelson expressed great confidence in his ability to overcome the Danish fire power with ten ships of the line. He was influenced by a feeling, which was prevalent in the fleet, that as the Danes had not been at war for eighty-five years, their gunnery would not be up to much. He underestimated the Danes' determination and the fact that they would be fighting on their own doorsteps; they were to give him the hardest-fought of all his battles.

On the afternoon of 30 March, the fleet anchored close to the north end of the outer deep and active preparations for the attack began. Except for a few battleships which were to remain in support under Hyde Parker's direct command, Nelson was to take charge of the whole fleet for the attack. He was to have ten ships of the line (later increased to twelve), the frigates, sloops, bomb vessels and all smaller craft; he transferred his flag to the *Elephant*, 74, since the extra draught of his second-rate, *St George*, would have been an unnecessarily risky handicap. His general idea was to take his ships down to the south end of the Holland Deep, then, as soon as the wind permitted, attack the Danish line in the King's Deep from the south. In this way he would avoid passing close to the formidable Trekroner battery at the north end of the Danish line. This was the first advantage; the second was that, as soon as a few ships at the south end could be silenced, he could bring his bomb vessels into the shallow water close to the south-east wall of the city.

Bomb vessels were highly specialised craft. Their hulls were strengthened to enable them to carry two heavy-calibre mortars, which could fire 13-inch shells over a short range with a high trajectory. Bomb vessels were therefore very effective in bombarding a target over intervening obstructions such as a spit of land or city walls.

To put this plan into operation, Nelson's ships had to navigate the Holland Deep. This was going to be risky as it was of limited depth, with mudbanks on either side and no channel markers. Part of the operation, therefore, was to lay marker buoys. During the afternoon and evening of the 30th, ships' carpenters were busy making buoys from empty barrels with two or three cannon balls for anchors. That night, boats crept off into the darkness and, by a triumph of methodical seamanship, succeeded in laying four buoys down the Swedish side of the deep.

On 31 March, Parker, still in the throes of anxiety, called a council of war. This was an official procedure whereby a commander could seek the views of the more senior of his subordinates. There may have been circumstances when its use was justifiable but it is hard to visualise what they might be. It was as good as a public announcement that the commander did not feel sure of himself, a very bad piece of psychology on the eve of a battle. It could have been used in some subsequent enquiry as evidence that what he did must have been reasonable, because his officers agreed with it; but Parker should have remembered Admiral Byng. About fifty years previously, Byng had held a council of war when he felt himself in an impossible situation; it did not stop the government of the day having him tried and shot as a smoke-screen to cover its own ineptitude. But, whatever his exact motives, Sir Hyde got together Nelson, Rear-Admiral Graves, and his captain of the fleet, Dommett, and asked them for their views on the propriety of attacking the enemy. In view of the apparent folly of such a question at that stage, it is surprising that Graves, a perfectly competent officer, advised against attack. He, at least, must have felt some of the doubts that were undermining Parker; however, he was outvoted by Nelson and Dommett and the attack was on.

Once the council of war had completed its deliberations, ships' boats again crept down the Holland Deep to lay buoys beyond those laid the night before. On the following day, 1 April, a signal was made from the *Elephant* requiring all masters and pilots to come aboard. (Pilots, many of whom were not naval personnel, had been brought along by most ships; they were of use in pointing out the dangers but, like most experts, were better at emphasising snags than suggesting how they might be overcome.) From *Elephant* they were all taken on a number of smaller craft which beat down the Holland Deep, sounding as they went, adding what they could to the information already gathered and familiarising the ships' masters with the channel.

By mid-afternoon the wind had become fair and Nelson's squadron weighed anchor. In line behind *Elephant* the battleships, frigates, sloops and bomb vessels sailed through the channel, aided by the buoys that had been laid and by the inspection carried out that morning; by the evening they had anchored south of the Middle Ground. From here they could sail north through the King's Deep as soon as the wind came round sufficiently to the south. Nelson was in buoyant mood as he dined that evening in the great cabin of *Elephant*; he had with him a number of old friends. Foley, *Elephant*'s captain, had been captain of *Goliath* and had led the attack at the Nile; Hardy, sometime captain of the brig *Mutine* now of *St Joseph* (not in Nelson's squadron) was present as a volunteer; Fremantle, of *Ganges*, had been with him in an abortive attack on Santa Cruz and at the successful capture of Bastia in Corsica in 1794. Also present were frigate captains Riou and Inman.

After the meal Riou, who was the senior frigate captain, remained aboard to help Nelson and Foley with the preparation of detailed orders and Hardy took a boat to do what surreptitious sounding he could along the King's Deep. Nelson was anxious to get his written orders completed and copied because he felt that the wind might back south before long, and as soon as it did he wanted to start the attack. His genius included 'an infinite capacity for taking pains'; he had been able to gain so much information about the Danish dispositions that he was able to include precise orders for each of his ships. Each captain was told the order in which he was to move off, the opponent he was to select and what to do once that opponent was subdued.

Nelson was about to attack over twenty moored vessels of various sorts with twelve ships of the line. As soon as any ship gained a victory, it was to move forward, leapfrogging any ships still engaged, and attack the next unengaged ship in the enemy line. Eventually, every Danish ship would be tackled. Smaller vessels were to keep out of direct fire and rake Danish vessels from the comparatively safe 'end-on' position as opportunity offered; bomb vessels were to shelter behind the ships of the line and shell the Trekroner Fort and the Danish arsenal, moving closer in to the town shore when the elimination of the enemy ships made this possible. Boats full of Marines were to shelter behind the flagship until the time came when it would be feasible for them to land. Riou, with his frigates, was ordered to 'perform such services as he is directed by the Vice-Admiral' – in other words to be ready for anything.

As dawn broke on 2 April 1801, the wind was coming south, fair for the King's Deep. At 7.00 a.m. all captains were called aboard *Elephant* and given their orders. This was followed by signals requiring all ships to prepare for anchoring by the stern, as had been done

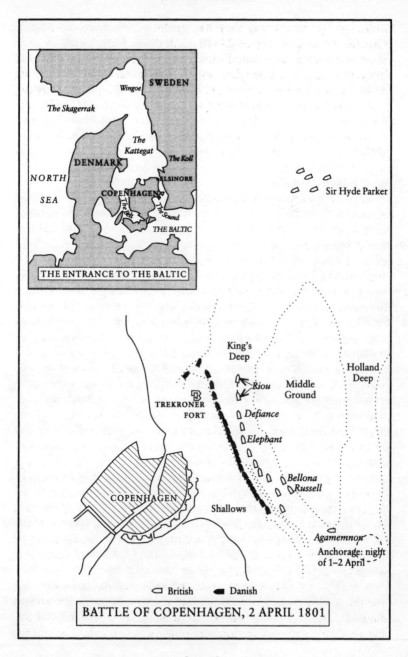

THE ENTRANCE TO THE BALTIC

Sir Hyde Parker

King's
Deep

Holland
Deep

Riou

Middle
Ground

TREKRONER
FORT

Defiance

Elephant

Bellona
Russell

COPENHAGEN

Shallows

Agamemnon

Anchorage: night
of 1–2 April

◁ British   ◀ Danish

BATTLE OF COPENHAGEN, 2 APRIL 1801

at the Nile. At about 10.00 a.m. the squadron was ordered to weigh; led by *Edgar*, the ships began to move north up King's Deep to their battle stations. Knowledge of the King's Deep was, of course, far from complete; it had not been possible to examine it like Holland Deep. As it turned out, the Middle Ground had an irregular edge on the King's Deep side – unexpected spurs of mud stuck out into the generally deeper water, which could take a ship by surprise even though the lead were in use. Three ships were caught in this way. The first was *Agamemnon*, Nelson's first wartime command, which ran aground on the southern tip of the Middle Ground; her assigned position had been alongside the first Danish ship and Nelson hastily relocated *Polyphemus* to her place. In a similar fashion, both *Bellona* and *Russell* grounded as they passed along the Danish line. Fortunately, they were both still able to engage, but at rather longer range than intended. At the south end of the King's Deep, in places there is a distinct outlying mudbank between the main channel and the shallow area to the west. This was encountered by Hardy during his overnight reconnaissance and it led to a belief that there might be a continuous shoal between the Danish line and the navigable part of the King's Deep. In consequence there was a tendency for the British ships to keep further away from the enemy line than they did, for example, at the Nile. The fear of a hazard between his ship and the enemy line would have been augmented by a captain's natural instinct to steer away from shallowing water indicated by the lead; the result was that as the squadron sounded its way up the channel, it gravitated towards the centre. So the whole battle was fought at longer range than was usual in close action; Colonel William Stewart, the commander of the troops carried by the fleet, recalled that the average distance between the lines was 200 yards.

The grounding of *Agamemnon*, *Bellona* and *Russell* had the effect of reducing the length of the Danish line which could be covered by the British battleships in the initial assault. Seeing this, and apparently on his own initiative, but without demur from Nelson, Captain Riou took his flotilla of frigates and sloops to the head of the squadron to lie in the line of battle, an unheard-of situation for lighter ships, and one of great danger because they came under fire from the Trekroner battery. Shore batteries were a menace to any ship, and especially formidable to frigates and sloops. Their only hope of survival was that they were a good half-mile away, within range but beyond the most accurate shooting.

Once battle was joined there was no manoeuvring and little science: it was simple, brutal slogging. The Danes were in a position to reinforce their vessels from the shore but, in practice, this was not likely to have been of much advantage to them. Guns were as likely to be hit as men and it is to be presumed that the battle started with the most experienced men in the crews. Severe damage to a gun or extensive slaughter among a gun crew could not rapidly be compensated for by an influx of inexperienced men. Aboard Nelson's ships there was no sail-handling or other sailing duties to be done, so they had a greater reserve than usual to replace casualties at the guns. It seems probable that the Danes did not enjoy much advantage from the proximity of the shore – except a possible moral one – but, as will be seen, there were attempts by shore parties to bring totally disabled vessels back into action. The deciding factor, almost certainly, was the standard of gunnery in which the British, unlike the Danes, had received constant training and practice. By shortly after noon, it was apparent that the Danish fire was beginning to slacken and one or two of the floating batteries had struck their flags, although the Danes still in action were fighting grimly.

London, Sir Hyde Parker's flagship, and four other ships remained, under his direct control, at the north end of the Middle Ground. The intention had been that they should move towards the town and support Nelson by firing, at long range, on the Trekroner Fort at the north end of the Danish line. In practice, their support amounted to little, as the south wind, which had enabled Nelson to move up the King's Deep, was dead foul for Sir Hyde. The support ships were therefore unable to get close enough to be effective and Sir Hyde had, perforce, to remain a long-range spectator.

At about 1.00 p.m. signal no. 39 was flown aboard *London*. Signal 39 in the Admiralty *Signal Book* of 1799 meant 'Discontinue the engagement' – a strange order to be made at the very moment when the first signs of success could be seen by those on the spot. The signal was reported to Nelson, who was walking his quarterdeck talking to Colonel Stewart. At first he said very little; on being asked if the signal should be repeated (that is, flown by his own flagship as an order to vessels under his command), he said 'No, acknowledge it.' A moment later he called after the signals officer, 'Is signal 16 [for close action] still flying?' On being told that it was, he said, 'Mind you keep it so,' and continued talking to Colonel Stewart. Later he made his famous gesture of putting his telescope to his blind eye and saying to Captain

Foley, 'You know, Foley, I have only one eye and I have a right to be blind sometimes – I really do not see the signal.' The battle continued; the only ships which complied with the order were the smaller vessels under Captain Riou and they did so on seeing it repeated by Rear-Admiral Graves. Admiral Graves was in duty bound to repeat the signal although he kept signal 16 flying and continued the action.

By early afternoon, most of the Danish vessels had stopped firing, whereas all British ships were still fit for action. Now there appeared from the shore parties of men who attempted to board floating batteries which had surrendered and to recommence firing from them. There was little possibility of their becoming a great threat but it was an action which could not be tolerated. The whole convention of mercy to surrendered ships would be endangered if a vessel, once surrendered, was likely to start firing again. Nelson therefore sent a message to the Danish command under a flag of truce:

> To the Brothers of Englishmen, the Danes.
> Lord Nelson has directions to spare Denmark, when no longer resisting; but if the firing is continued on the part of Denmark, Lord Nelson will be obliged to set on fire all the Floating-batteries he has taken, without having the power of saving the brave Danes who have defended them. Dated on board His Britannick Majesty's ship Elephant, Copenhagen Roads, April 2nd, 1801.

This was effectively the end of the battle; the exchanges following Nelson's note led to negotiations which eventually resulted in an armistice ratified by the government in London. Before confirmation of the government's approval reached the Baltic, word came to Sir Hyde Parker that Tsar Paul of Russia had died on 24 March (well before the battle), and that the new tsar, Alexander I, was anxious to establish friendly relations with Britain. In fact, the treaty of armed neutrality was a dead letter and the battle need never have been fought; but, with the communications then available, nobody could have known that. To dwell on this fact is as unprofitable as pondering the possibility that, had Parker been a little more prompt, the Danes might have given in without a battle; or that, had the fleet gone through the Belt and made for the Russian fleet, the Russians would not have fought because of the death of the tsar. Nevertheless, the government considered that Parker had not shown up well, and the same dispatch which brought approval of the armistice brought his recall to London. This was probably just, although it represented judgement on the basis of a higher standard than had been applied to some admirals in the past.

So, in spite of all Sir Hyde's caution, his conduct was not approved after all. He was neither self-confident nor lucky and his hesitations are understandable as those of a man overawed by the complexities of his task. What is harder to understand, at first glance, is why he flew signal 39 in the middle of the battle. Everybody knows about Nelson putting his telescope to his blind eye but, until recently, there was a strange lack of curiosity about why the signal to discontinue the action was made.

There have been various theories about this, which boil down to the following three. First, that the signal had been pre-arranged between Sir Hyde and Nelson to give the latter an honourable way out if he thought the battle was going badly; second, that there was no prior arrangement, but Sir Hyde made the signal to give Nelson the opportunity to withdraw if he needed it, expecting that he would otherwise ignore it; and, third, that the signal was made because Sir Hyde feared Nelson was getting the worst of the battle, and in disregard of the probable disastrous consequences had the ships tried to turn from the action, under fire from an undefeated enemy and in a narrow channel with shallows close at hand.

The first theory emanated from a Lieutenant-Colonel Hutchinson, who commanded a detachment of troops on board *London*. No solid grounds emerge for his supposition and there are a number of objections to it. It can probably be safely discounted.

The second theory was introduced by the poet Robert Southey, in his biography of Nelson. He states it as a fact, as one who is glad to put the record straight, but gives no source. His words carry some weight because his brother, Tom Southey, was in the battle. Unfortunately, Tom Southey was wounded aboard *Bellona*, aground on the mud at the south end of King's Deep and could not have known much about the motives of the commander-in-chief on his flagship five miles away.

Modern historians have given more weight to the third theory, mainly on the grounds that the signal was made 'general', i.e. addressed to all ships and not personally to Nelson (as could have been done under the applicable signal code). Stress is laid on the chaos which would have followed if all Nelson's ships had tried to obey the order simultaneously. The signal is written off as Parker's last, and potentially worst, mistake, which escaped causing disaster only because nobody chose to obey it (except for the frigates and sloops under Riou).

Yet there are substantial objections to the third theory. Riou and his smaller ships obeyed signal 39 because, in his position to the north of the line of battleships, he could see both Parker's flagship, *London*, and Rear-Admiral Graves' flagship, *Defiance*, which was the north-ernmost ship of the line; he could not see signals on Nelson's flagship, *Elephant*. His frigates and sloops had taken up an emergency position, in which they were taking a battering for which they were not designed, and which they could not sustain for long. Consequently, when Riou saw Parker's signal repeated by the nearest senior officer, there was no reason for him to hesitate, especially as he was in com-paratively open water, where it was practicable to retire.

The case of the battleships in touch with Nelson, and under his command, was totally different. It would be an unheard-of thing, in any disciplined service, for commanders to carry out a general order, in battle, without reference to their immediate senior commander. Whatever the letter of naval law of the time, it would have been contrary to all military experience. It is inconceivable that ships in Nelson's squadron would have turned away and left the action with-out reference to him. If it were conceivable, why did Nelson take no steps to stop it? He need not have dramatically cancelled the C-in-C's order – he only had to signal the equivalent of 'Wait'. Yet he did no such thing, but only asked if signal 16 were still flying. It is clear that, unless and until Nelson hauled down his signal for close action and replaced it with another, nothing dramatic would happen. The idea that Parker's signal could have led to an undisciplined and cata-strophic rush away from the battle has, therefore, no foundation.

It was in keeping with the flamboyant side of Nelson's character that he should afterwards dramatise the situation by putting the tele-scope to his blind eye and referring to having fought 'against orders' – this was an understandable bit of showmanship. In hard fact, it was entirely proper for Nelson to ignore the signal to break off action; he was the commander on the spot and could assess the situation infi-nitely better than Sir Hyde Parker four or five miles away. Senior officers are paid to take responsibility, and not for one moment could Nelson's duty be interpreted as blind obedience to an order which was clearly based on insufficient knowledge of the situation.

This being so, it would have been perfectly in order for Sir Hyde

Parker to have flown the signal; he would know that Nelson would not comply if it were the wrong thing to do. He would, in fact, have been offering to take from Nelson's shoulders the heavy responsibility of breaking off the action if that had been necessary. It would have been an act showing moral courage and a proper sense of a senior commander's duty.

It may be that signal 39 was made in a panic and that, but for the merciful unanimity of thought on the part of the captains, all would have ended in disaster. To believe that, however, one has to believe that the order being made general overrode the invariable and instinctive practice of looking to one's immediate commander to control and co-ordinate any move in battle. One also has to believe that Nelson, knowing that all the ships around him might cut their cables and leave the scene (with collisions and groundings as an inevitable result), took no action at all to direct or inform them. It is physically possible but it does seem rather unlikely.

On the other hand, there is nothing particularly unlikely in the possibility that the commander-in-chief, seeing that his ships were hard pressed, and unable himself to get upwind to the scene, took the responsibility for a possible retreat; doing this in the knowledge that Nelson would not act on his signal were it unnecessary and that the ships under Nelson would not move until the order were confirmed by him. In other words, it does seem that Sir Hyde Parker, giving the final battle order of his career, at last did something right.

CHAPTER 9

Other Events, 1793–1802

Any account of the activities of the ships of the line must be concerned chiefly with the great sea battles. Almost by definition this was their designed function. Yet the battles were only brief highlights in their continuous duty; most of the time they influenced events just by their existence. In some spheres this was achieved by fleets – as in the blockade of the major French ports; in others one ship had the desired effect. Wherever there was a force of one or more ships of the line, the French could do nothing of note unless they could produce a stronger force.

During the Napoleonic wars, there were British ships of the line in the West Indies, the Mediterranean, the South Atlantic, the Indian Ocean and the China Sea (the two latter were referred to as the East Indies Station) as well as in the waters around Britain. They might go for years without opening their gunports in anger; but their presence meant that any enemy activity could only be hasty and furtive. Occasionally they were challenged and there were actions between small numbers of ships. These may not have been on the same scale as the major battles but they were all part of the same strategy – keeping the seas open for Britain and denying them to the enemy.

One of Britain's first warlike actions was the dispatch, on 24 March 1793, of seven battleships to the West Indies. It was hoped that the French possessions in the Caribbean would be pro-royalist and that, in the presence of a substantial British force, they would submit without resistance. This proved to be a false hope. Eight months later a second expedition under Sir John Jervis included troops, and warfare continued in the West Indies for most of the Revolutionary war. It led to heavy losses from disease for no great advantage to the British cause, but involved no naval actions between ships of the line.

A major success might have been achieved if as much attention had been given to the Mediterranean. There, in Toulon – the French naval port second only to Brest – the citizens had rebelled against the revolutionary government, presenting Britain with a ready-made beach-head opening a way to the heart of France. In August 1793 Admiral Hood anchored in Toulon harbour, trapping about thirty French ships of the line. France had many internal problems at the time, and a properly equipped army, sent to back up Hood's seamen and marines, could well have secured a firm foothold. But, apart from the arrival of a contingent of Neapolitan troops, nothing was done. The scratch forces in Toulon held out for four months; they were defeated in December 1793, after a certain Major Napoleon Bonaparte took over the command of the besieging artillery. Hood and his ships had to withdraw so hastily that fifteen French ships of the line were left undamaged to form the future French Mediterranean fleet.

Nelson was under Hood's command at this time, as captain of the 64-gun *Agamemnon*. During the siege of Toulon he was sent with orders to ships off Sardinia and, *en route*, met four French frigates, to which he gave chase. He caught up with the rearmost one, *Melpomène*. *Melpomène*, instead of surrendering, which would have been the normal and perfectly honourable thing to do when confronted with so superior a force, bravely resisted. Broadsides were exchanged and *Melpomène* was heavily damaged. However, *Agamemnon* was also temporarily disabled and unable to get close enough to enforce surrender. The three other French frigates turned and came back to the scene, but instead of tackling the damaged *Agamemnon* they contented themselves with assisting *Melpomène* to withdraw. One frigate could not be expected to fight a 64-gun ship, but three well-handled frigates could certainly have tackled one in damaged condition. Had they done so, Nelson might well have been killed or captured, which would have been a sad blow to the development of the Royal Navy. This is yet another example of the inconsistency in French performances, resulting from the lack of incisive high-level leadership; one frigate had the dash and courage to take on a ship of the line, then three of them failed to take the opportunity of beating her.

On withdrawing from Toulon, Hood took up his station in Hyères Bay, a short way along the coast to the east. He now had no adequate shore base in the western Mediterranean, and it was necessary to establish one if Toulon were to be properly watched. This was provided by the invasion of Corsica. The Corsicans were then in a state of rebellion against France and friendly to Britain, but the key points on the island were occupied by French troops. The navy was largely responsible for dislodging them, and Nelson lost his right eye in attacking Calvi. By August 1794 the navy could operate from San Fiorenza Bay (now known as Golfe de St-Florent), as well as Leghorn (Livorno) and La Spezia on the Italian coast.

The year 1794 also saw the battle of the Glorious First of June, after which the British Channel Fleet tended to keep to Spithead. Isolated cruises were made from time to time, but not often enough to keep a constant watch on the French, or with enough ships to restrict their movements. The dangers of employing ships in European waters in penny numbers were demonstrated in November 1794 when *Canada* and *Alexander*, both 74s, met five French battleships about 200 miles west of Ushant. *Alexander* was taken but *Canada* got away to take the news to Lord Bridport (then second in command of the Channel fleet). Lord Bridport did, then, take the fleet to sea, but within three weeks he returned to Spithead, where the fleet stayed for the rest of the year and well into 1795.

One result of the inadequate blockade was that the French were able to send troops to the West Indies. There were some British ships of the line in the Indies, but French convoys of troop-carrying vessels were getting through. The British were forced on to the defensive. In November 1795 a substantial convoy carrying 16,000 troops under General Abercromby, escorted by eight ships of the line under Admiral Christian, left Spithead for Barbados. On the 17th, winds of hurricane force swept up the Channel. One transport got through, and eventually arrived at Barbados; of the rest, some foundered and the survivors were driven back to Spithead. A second attempt was made early in December with results nearly as bad. General Abercromby finally got to Barbados in a frigate on 17 March 1796. Admiral Christian arrived a month later with the troopships. After this, Britain began to regain the initiative in the West Indies and, by and large, retained it thereafter.

In the winter of 1794–5, while the Channel Fleet was safely in Spithead, the French navy suffered terribly from the power of the sea. The worst of the Terror was over by the end of 1794 but France was still ruled by the Committee of Public Safety, with which none dared argue. It was decided, by the Committee, to take advantage of the absence of the Royal Navy from the eastern Atlantic, and send six ships of the line from Brest to Toulon. Admiral Villaret de Joyeuse, who had saved the grain convoy on the First of June, was to command an escort of thirty-five ships to shepherd the Toulon-bound six through the Bay of Biscay. On the face of it, a perfectly sound scheme; but what Villaret knew, and what he could not get the government to accept, was that the ships in Brest were in bad condition. Their summer activities had taken their toll and supplies for maintenance and refurbishing were not available. The ships were in need of naval stores, food and trained men. It was not reasonable to expect a force of forty-odd ships, based on Brest, to put to sea in midwinter. But the government, which was deaf to the navy's needs, insisted; and there was no appeal. The six ships for Toulon were equipped only by taking stores away from the other ships in the fleet; those in the escort were reduced to stores for a bare four weeks. This left very little margin for unforeseen delays – it took nearly a week for the whole fleet to get out of Brest.

By 1 January 1795 the fleet was at sea; it immediately ran into a strong gale, which set the scene for a continuing period of foul weather. Two 80-gun ships and one 74 foundered, two 74s ran ashore, and one first-rate was sinking. The stores of the escorting ships ran out and they could survive only by cannibalising the stores of those bound for Toulon. The transfer of stores by boat was, in itself, a desperate undertaking at sea in heavy weather; it also meant that none of the ships had enough stores left to go as far as Toulon. The survivors got back to Brest early in February. On their way back, when the worst of the weather had abated, they were able to redeem the situation by taking a number of merchant ships as prizes, but five ships of the line were lost. A few weeks later, the six ships destined for Toulon set out again and got there, unhampered by Bridport's Channel Fleet or by the Mediterranean Fleet, now based in Corsica.

In July 1795 Admiral George Elphinstone, commanding a squadron including four ships of the line, took the Cape of Good Hope from the Dutch with little opposition and without any sea battle. A Dutch squadron was sent to recover the Cape, but by the time it arrived Elphinstone had been reinforced and the Dutch had no hope of beating him. The Dutch admiral accepted the inevitable and surrendered. Admiral Elphinstone became Lord Keith as a result; an elevation fairly painlessly earned but, in later years, he showed up as a good admiral who deserved the honour as much as most.

In the Indian Ocean there were a number of combined operations against French outposts in the East Indies, in which ships of the line were not heavily involved.

In European waters, the absence of a tight blockade allowed the French and their allies to use the seas fairly freely. The French were able to sail between Brest and Toulon, and the Dutch were able to put to sea with little hindrance. A number of comparatively small-scale actions took place as a result.

On 8 June 1795, Admiral Villaret de Joyeuse was in the Bay of Biscay with three ships of the line, this time having the straightforward task of convoying coasters from Bordeaux to ports in the north. He was unfortunate enough to meet five British ships of the line, who took eight of his coasters, but Villaret and his warships got away to Brest. At Brest he was reinforced by nine ships and sailed again. On the 16th, his twelve ships of the line met the same five British ships and it was now the turn of the British to flee. On the following day the French gained on their quarry and a running battle developed which lasted all day. In the event, no ship was captured or seriously damaged. This has been held up as another example of inadequate French gunnery, which is hardly fair. In normal battle conditions ships were under a minimum area of sail and moving slowly; the guns could be handled in accordance with practised gun drill and some attempt at controlled aiming could be made. In the conditions of a general chase, pursuers and pursued would be sailing as fast as they could, with the maximum sail they could carry; the movement of the gundeck would not be a gentle heaving but a violent and probably irregular motion. To load, run up and fire a gun at all would be an achievement, never mind attempts at accuracy. In the event, neither side did any serious damage. At the end of the day the chase was abandoned.

Five days later the same twelve French ships met Lord Bridport with fourteen ships of the line, on a routine cruise off the south Brittany coast. Odds of 12:14 may not seem very long in a sea battle but Villaret was well aware that the state of his ships and the standard of his crews made the odds, in practice, very much greater. He, very sensibly, made for the safety of Lorient harbour, the entrance to which lies behind the Île de Groix. Once again, there was a long chase, which lasted throughout the night and into the next day, 23 June 1795. That day the British caught up with the tail of the French fleet and three ships of the line were captured, including *Alexander*, which had been

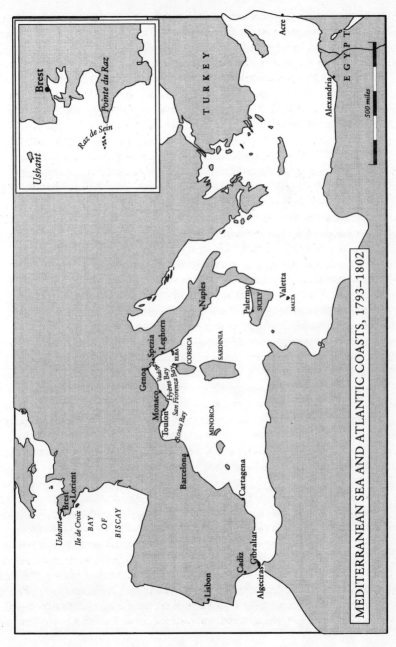

MEDITERRANEAN SEA AND ATLANTIC COASTS, 1793–1802

taken by the French the previous November, and *Tigre*, which was to be captained by Sidney Smith at Acre.

Meanwhile, Villaret de Joyeuse and the remaining nine French ships had reached the inshore side of the Île de Groix, but could not get into Lorient harbour until the tide had risen. Lord Bridport looked at the nine French ships, now waiting at the mercy of his fourteen, and thought of the rocky shore and shoaling water, for which he had only sketchy charts. He thought of the three ships already taken, not by any standards a bad result, and decided to hold back. The British watched the tide rise and Villaret de Joyeuse sail into harbour and safety. At the time the action was hailed, naturally, as a glorious victory for Bridport. Later in the war it would have been thought that where nine French ships could go fourteen British ships could, and must, follow, and that none should have escaped. Lord Bridport's caution was typical of the more deliberate approach current in 1795.

The outlook of Admiral William Hotham, then commander-in-chief of the Mediterranean, was very similar, and Nelson was already fretting about it. Word had reached Hotham, based on Leghorn, that the fifteen French ships of the line, left behind in Toulon when Hood pulled out in December 1793, were at sea. On 9 March 1795, Hotham left Leghorn with thirteen ships to seek them out. He soon found that they were off Corsica and had taken *Berwick*, 74, which had been alone in San Fiorenza Bay. On 11 March the French were sighted to windward, making for Toulon. They continued to head for Toulon while Hotham gave chase, with Captain Nelson in *Agamemnon* leading. With the pursuit at its height the two rearmost French ships collided and *Ça Ira* fell out of the line with a damaged bowsprit and foremast. Nelson opened fire on *Ça Ira* but, as he was alone, well ahead of the body of the fleet, he was driven off by the ships coming back to her assistance. *Ça Ira* was taken in tow by *Censeur* and the chase continued.

The pursuit continued throughout the night and in the morning *Ça Ira* and *Censeur* were seen to have fallen far behind the rest of the French fleet and their capture was imminent. However, the British had first to occupy themselves with the French main body which had turned back. The two fleets passed each other on opposite tacks, and the British got rather the worst of the exchange of fire, but they succeeded in keeping the French fleet away from *Ça Ira* and *Censeur*. The French, already reduced in strength, avoided a pitched battle and stood off. After a gallant resistance, *Ça Ira* and *Censeur* were taken.

Greatly to Nelson's annoyance, Hotham then called off the chase, saying, 'We must be contented, we have done very well.' In a subsequent letter to his wife, Nelson said, 'Had we taken 10 sail and allowed the 11th to have escaped . . . I could never call it well done.' The day would come when Hotham's outlook would be discredited and Nelson's accepted, but that day was not yet.

Whatever the rights and wrongs of the action, the French had been driven away from Corsica and, for the moment, they abandoned plans for its recapture. Admiral Hotham was joined by Rear-Admiral Robert Man with six additional ships of the line, and was now fairly well established, based on Corsica and Leghorn. At this time (the second half of 1795), the Austrians were advancing in northern Italy and Hotham's main task was to give them support.

Around the northern shores of the Mediterranean, the mountains come down close to the sea, with very little in the way of a littoral plain. This meant that the only roads available were poor-quality tracks, between the sea and the mountains, vulnerable to attack from the sea. The best way to move heavy stores was by ship. It would thus have been of great advantage to the advancing Austrians to have a naval force to protect both the left flank of their army and the passage of their army's supplies by coastal craft.

It would have been of great advantage, that is to say, had the naval campaign of protection and assistance been pursued with vigour and imagination. Unfortunately, Hotham was neither aggressive nor imaginative. In his letters to his wife, Fanny, Nelson frequently referred to the lack-lustre manner in which the Mediterranean fleet was being managed. For example, on 1 September 1795 he wrote, 'I am almost afraid, from the inactivity of our Admiral, that the campaign in this country will end in a very different manner to what might have been expected.' And on 5 October 1795: 'How different would our situation have been if that great officer, Lord Hood [had] been out here. I am almost certain we should at this moment have possessed all Provence.'

During the autumn of 1795 six French ships of the line and three frigates sailed from Hyères, with a Captain Richery as commodore, bound for North America. Hotham learned of their departure on 22 September, but did not take positive action until 6 October. On that date he dispatched Rear-Admiral Man with six ships of the line in pursuit. Man eventually bottled up Richery in Cadiz but not before he had taken a British convoy and one 74-gun ship of the escort.

In November Sir John Jervis arrived to take over from Hotham and standards in the Mediterranean Fleet began to improve. Too late, however, for the Austrians, who had lost momentum. A few months later Napoleon began his first victorious campaign in northern Italy.

The story of 1796 in the Mediterranean is one of steady progress by the French in northern Italy in spite of Jervis. Had he been on the scene during the Austrian advance, his vigorous support might have helped it to more lasting success. Once the Austrians were in retreat, nothing he and the fleet could do was sufficient to stem the tide now flowing in favour of Napoleon and his Army of Italy. The year ended with the withdrawal of the British from the Mediterranean.

In the East Indies command, two 74-gun ships, *Victorious* and *Arrogant*, had been in action against a number of French frigates. The action was indecisive, in that there were no losses of ships on either side, but it achieved the objective of preventing a French assault on Penang. Otherwise activity was chiefly against privateers, which were still taking a number of merchant ships in the Indian Ocean. In the West Indies the majority of islands were now in British hands, things were slowing down, and naval activity was generally confined to smaller vessels than ships of the line.

The events of late 1796 and 1797 in Europe are described in Chapters 5 and 6. In the West Indies, Trinidad was taken, leaving only Guadeloupe, Puerto Rico and some smaller Dutch islands in enemy hands. In the Indian Ocean, French action against India, following the evacuation by Britain of the Mediterranean, began to appear a serious possibility. Ships from the East Indies station were occupied in keeping watch, as far as possible, on Red Sea ports which might have been utilised by the French had they got that far. An expedition by the British East Indies squadron to the Philippines to take Manila from Spain was proposed; this was abandoned so that all resources should be available for the possible defence of India. The situation remained much the same throughout 1798 until the news of the battle of the Nile came through.

In the most distant stations, the West and East Indies, there was little dramatic activity affecting the big ships after 1797, right up to the Peace of Amiens in 1802. The ships of the line in these areas fulfilled their purpose by limiting the options available to the enemy. They might send fast frigates; if they could, and the scale of events had justified it, the French might have sent a battle fleet. But they

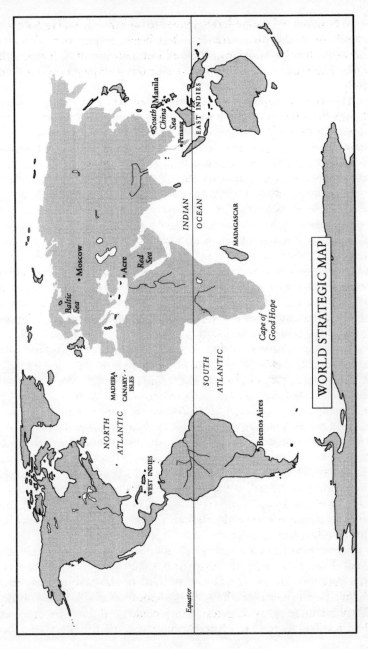

South China Sea
Manila
EAST INDIES
Penang

INDIAN OCEAN

MADAGASCAR

Moscow • Acre • Red Sea

Baltic Sea

Cape of Good Hope

MADEIRA
CANARY ISLES

NORTH ATLANTIC

SOUTH ATLANTIC

Buenos Aires

WEST INDIES

Equator

WORLD STRATEGIC MAP

were deterred from attempting any medium-scale operations by the presence of the British battleships.

In European and Mediterranean waters the years 1798 and 1799 were full of incident although, after the Nile, there were no battles much larger than single-ship actions. Nelson's fleet dispersed; a few ships were left to blockade Alexandria, a number went back to St Vincent with the French prizes and Nelson went to Naples. The 50-gun *Leander* was sent off on her own, ahead of the others, to take the news of the battle to St Vincent and was unfortunate enough to fall in with *Généreux*, the French 74 which had escaped. *Leander* was taken after a spirited defence.

The main preoccupations in the Mediterranean became: a blockade of Malta, where the French were still holding out in Valetta; bolstering up Britain's only Mediterranean ally, the Kingdom of Naples (which included Sicily); and the taking of Minorca from Spain.

Nearer home, another attempt was made against Ireland, which in 1798 was on the brink of full-scale rebellion. A French brigade under General Humbert succeeded in landing in Killaly Bay on the west coast. At various times during the wars, both sides made the mistake of thinking that a weak invading force could survive if the local inhabitants were friendly. It was, in each case, fatal; an invading force must be able both to provide for itself from its own resources and, at the same time, to defeat the defending forces with its own strength. A brigade was not enough and General Humbert's men were soon rounded up and captured.

The naval squadron which had transported General Humbert sailed as soon as his troops were landed and returned safely to France. A second squadron carrying additional troops was not so fortunate. It consisted of the 74-gun *Hoche* (named after the general in command of the troops in the previous attempt on Ireland and who might have become one of France's greatest heroes if he had not died at the age of twenty-nine in 1797) and eight frigates. It was caught off the north coast of Ireland by Sir John Borlase Warren with three ships of the line and five frigates. Of the nine French ships, only two frigates got back to France; *Hoche* was taken and, with her, the Irish patriot Wolfe Tone. He was an honourable man, who had committed himself totally to what he believed in; he refused a chance to transfer to a frigate, in which he might have escaped, and subsequently died by his own hand in prison.

In 1799 there was a major naval crisis of which little has been heard because, in the end, no dramatic results ensued. Nevertheless, it involved extensive fleet activity and could have ended in another great naval battle. It did not do so, Lord Keith missed the chance of becoming a major naval hero, and the crisis was contained with no harm done. The way this was achieved illustrates an improvement in the efficiency of senior commanders since the winter of 1796–7, and forms a significant part of the story of the ships of the line.

By 1799 the blockade of French ports was being more systematically applied and in April Lord Bridport, C-in-C of the Channel Fleet, with sixteen ships of the line, took over the blockade of Brest. On the 24th it could be seen that a number of ships within Brest roads had their yards in place with sails bent on ready for sea. The wind was north-east, and Lord Bridport took up a position about twelve miles south-west of Ushant. By pre-St Vincent standards, it was a perfectly sound position; in the wind prevailing, the French, when they came out, were bound to pass within reach of Bridport's position. Unless of course, they turned sharply south, on emerging from the Goulet de Brest, and went through the Raz de Sein. The Raz de Sein is a fairly narrow channel through the rocks lying off the headland, Pointe du Raz, about fifteen miles south of Brest. By using it a vessel can cut out the long detour to sea which, when heading south, is otherwise necessary to avoid the rocks; but great caution is called for in doing so. The tidal currents are swift; in any strength of wind the seas can be dangerous, and the Raz de Sein is not infrequently shrouded in mist. It is a place which requires accurate timing and considerable respect, even in the days of reliable engines and radar; not a prudent route through which to take twenty-five ships of the line. This, however, is exactly what Admiral Bruix did.

On 25 April, while Bridport waited, quietly confident, thirty miles away, Bruix took twenty-five line ships and ten smaller vessels through the Raz de Sein, and disappeared into the haze to the south. He was seen by a British frigate on inshore patrol. Ideally there should have been enough frigates inshore to keep in touch with the French as well as getting a message back to Bridport. Unfortunately this was not the case; the inshore frigate passed the message to Bridport but, in doing so, lost sight of the enemy. The French could be anywhere; they could be pressing on to the south and the Mediterranean, they could be heading south and then west into the Atlantic, or they could be heading south, then west, then north to the Channel or to Ireland.

Lord Bridport cannot be blamed too severely for losing the French

– it had happened before and was to happen again, even to Nelson. What mattered now was the way in which he dealt with this difficult situation. His actions certainly indicate that he was determined not to be caught out again as he had been in December 1796, when the French arrived off Bantry Bay and his fleet was trapped in Spithead. He decided that the place to be covered at all costs was Ireland, and thither he took his sixteen battleships. But at the same time he provided for other possibilities. First he sent messages to the Channel ports, warning of the situation, and ordering all ships which could to get to sea and rally to him. At the same time he sent messages to St Vincent at Gibraltar and Keith off Cadiz. All he could do thereafter was to wait until he received further news, meanwhile his ships were at sea, and ready to go wherever the trouble should develop.

Lord Bridport had so far done well; he was, perhaps, a little slow in coming to his next decision, in that it was 1 June before he decided that the threat lay elsewhere and detached twelve ships to join St Vincent, then C-in-C in the Mediterranean. Nevertheless, the ships were sent; the fleet was at sea and not in Spithead and, when it was decided to send them to the Mediterranean, the ships were already well on the way there.

Meanwhile, the French had continued on their way south, and on 3 May arrived off Cadiz, where Lord Keith, now second in command to St Vincent, with fifteen ships of the line, was hanging on to his blockading station in a north-west gale. It was a stalemate; the Spaniards in Cadiz could not get out because of Lord Keith; for fear of letting the Spaniards out Lord Keith could not leave his station to take on the French; the French, in spite of their superior numbers, did not wish to attack Lord Keith because he was on a lee shore. Operations on a lee shore must always be attended by risk, experience and seamanship are at a premium. To start an attack, on a lee shore, with crews undoubtedly less experienced and well trained than those of one's opponent, would be the height of folly. Bruix thought of all this and sailed on, passing Gibraltar on 5 May.

Lord St Vincent, who was not in the best of health, was ashore in Gibraltar to watch the French go by. There was still no firm indication of their purpose, but St Vincent had no doubt about where the greatest danger lay. If the French managed to combine with the Spanish fleet in Cartagena, the combined fleet would be so large that, even allowing for disparities in efficiency, his own ships, scattered in small numbers about the Mediterranean, would be in dire peril. To combine his ships, and prevent them being destroyed piecemeal, he would risk everything else; he would risk the Spanish getting out of Cadiz, the loss of Minorca (recently taken from the Spanish), the relief of Malta, or even the relief of the French army, cut off from France in Egypt. All these situations could be dealt with in due course, if he could first dispose of the massive threat confronting him. He sent messages to Keith at Cadiz and Nelson at Palermo; Keith was to join him but Nelson was to stay put for the moment.

On 20 May 1799 St Vincent was at Minorca, having combined the ships already there under Commodore John Duckworth with Keith's squadron which had now joined him. Here he received the further news he desperately needed to enable him to decide what to do next; the French had been seen north of Minorca, obviously on their way to Toulon. They had not paused at Cartagena but, on the other hand, the Spaniards there had been joined by the ships recently held by Keith in Cadiz. Now, although much was uncertain, he knew where the Spanish were and, for the moment, where the French were. He therefore took his ships to the Spanish coast north-west of Barcelona, whence he could follow the French if they went further east, or intercept them if they tried to go back and join the Spaniards at Cartagena. On 30 May he heard that the French had left Toulon, and shortly afterwards he was joined by the first five of the ships sent to join him from the United Kingdom.

Admiral Bruix might be going to relieve Malta, he might be going to Egypt or he might be going to Sicily. It was fairly certain that he had not doubled back towards Cartagena. St Vincent headed north-east to follow cautiously. He wanted to keep his fleet substantially intact for when he should catch up with Bruix but, with the reinforcement he had now received, he could hedge his bets to a certain extent. He dared not turn south-west with his whole fleet in an attempt to intercept the French, in case they should turn back and dodge behind him to Cartagena; but he was now in a position, with great caution, to spread his resources a little. He sent four ships under Duckworth to Nelson at Palermo. At this point he fell ill and had to hand over to Lord Keith.

St Vincent went back in a small craft to Minorca, and Keith continued north-east in the track of the French. On 5 June he had word that they had been seen in Vado Bay near Genoa so he was still in a sound position, in pursuit and still blocking any retreat to Cartagena. He was passing Monaco, not far behind the French, when the wind changed. It now blew from the east, dead foul for his pursuit of the French, but a fair wind from their last position to either Sicily or Minorca. Keith detached two further ships to join Nelson in Sicily, just in case. He was personally convinced, however, that the French would go to Minorca, which they could reach without meeting the British fleet, where they could do a lot of damage, and where they could easily receive support from the Spaniards in Cartagena.

At this point an order from St Vincent reached Keith, requiring him to abandon the pursuit of the French and revert to lying in wait off Rosas Bay, just south of the Franco-Spanish border. He obeyed the order to the extent that he abandoned the pursuit and fell back to the west but, convinced that his own appreciation of the situation was the right one, he went to Minorca instead of Rosas Bay.

Lord Keith was wrong and his senior admiral was right. From the beginning St Vincent's aim had been simple – never mind anything else, keep the French and Spaniards apart; and if Keith had done as he was told, he would have kept between the two enemy fleets and found himself squarely in Bruix's path. For Bruix had abandoned other plans and turned before the east wind to run back towards Cartagena, passing Rosas Bay where Keith would have been watching if he had kept away from Minorca.

Fortunately for Keith, no evil consequences followed the junction of the French and Spanish fleets. British reinforcements had by now reached the Mediterranean, and Bruix, instead of coming back with a large combined fleet, carried on with the minimum of delay for Brest. As soon as this news reached Minorca on 10 July, Keith set off in pursuit. He was something like a week behind when he left but, by the time the pursuit had reached Brest, Bruix got into harbour with barely twenty-four hours to spare.

It is interesting to note that no retribution was visited on Lord Keith for his mistake. He was the commander on the spot; had things gone well as a result of his decision, like Nelson at St Vincent and Copenhagen he would have been considered fully justified in backing his judgement. As it was, he was perhaps fortunate not to be criticised, although he might not have escaped censure if some disaster had resulted. Nevertheless, let nobody think he went unpunished. Lord Keith was a competent commander and went on to hold high office for many years, but in all his career he never fought a battle. When he looked back in his old age, it must have been a galling thought that, if he had not made that misjudgement, or if it had been discovered twenty-four hours earlier, his name might have been up there with those of Howe, Nelson and the others.

Whatever individual shortcomings there may have been, the crisis was handled rather better than that of 1796–7, when Ireland was threatened. Decisions were made, information was sent to the right places, ships stayed at sea, and fleets combined, as necessary, to provide a force powerful enough to handle whatever might transpire. As it happened, the whole thing passed off harmlessly, but if the French timing had been better, and if they had found more helpful weather, the danger could have been very much greater.

At about the same time as Admiral Bruix was slipping through the Raz de Sein (the end of April 1799), matters were coming to a head at the far end of the Mediterranean. The battle of the Nile had brought to an end all French movement in the Mediterranean; Napoleon was cut off from France and any further seaborne supplies, but he had one more card to play. If he could get his army across the Sinai desert to Syria and Asia Minor before strong forces were assembled against him, he still had a chance. With the Ottoman Empire brought to heel, he could establish overland contact with France through the Balkans, and his great eastern adventure was still a possibility. By the latter end of April he had crossed the desert and was investing Acre, a strong point on the coast of Palestine and the last obstacle.

He had to take Acre; otherwise, with the British in the Mediterranean, it would have been a fatal danger to his flank and rear. Acre, however, was a tougher problem than expected. The British government had shown considerable prescience in sending a mission to the Turks, hot on the heels of Nelson's fleet. This mission consisted mainly of John Spencer Smith, a diplomat, and his brother, Captain Sir Sidney Smith, in the 80-gun *Tigre*. Sir Sidney Smith was one of history's great characters; he was brave, enthusiastic and unconventional, and he knew how to get on with the Turks. When the threat to Acre became apparent, Sir Sidney in *Tigre*, supported by the Nile veteran Captain Miller in *Theseus*, responded. He had with him a number of small gunboats and a formidable array of helpers, in particular Colonel Phelippeaux, a French Royalist officer who was an experienced military engineer.

The Turks were brave fighters, though undisciplined and cruel to infidels. Their technology, however, was medieval, not to say primitive. Alone, they would have had little hope against Napoleon's hardened troops. But, seasoned by the addition of Sidney Smith's resources, they were a very different proposition. Colonel Phelip-peaux organised scientific defence lines and clear fields of fire; he taught them how to counter the besiegers' field works and how to deal with mining. The ships provided the disciplined musketry of the Marines as well as guns and gunners. Some guns and their crews were brought ashore to augment Acre's defences; most remained aboard so that the ships' broadsides could be used against attackers. Besides all this, Sir Sidney's men captured a coastal convoy of small craft bringing siege guns to Napoleon; the defenders were thus given extra time to make preparations for receiving the assault, while Napoleon was replacing the guns.

Consequently, instead of taking Acre in his stride, Napoleon was locked into the siege for two months. At last, on 20 May 1799, having made no progress, and with ships full of Turkish reinforcements on the way, he had to give up and return to Egypt. On 20 May, Admiral Bruix was in the western Mediterranean heading for Toulon; had he started his enterprise a month earlier and had he been lucky, he might just have reached the shore of Palestine while the siege of Acre was still in progress. However closely Lord Keith had been following, and whatever the outcome of the subsequent naval battle, Sir Sidney's efforts could well have been countered for just long enough. Napoleon would have achieved his foothold in the East.

This did not happen, however, and, while the rest of the navy shepherded Admiral Bruix back to Brest, *Tigre* and *Theseus* could claim that they had been instrumental in stopping Napoleon at the farthest point from France he ever reached.

From 1799 to 1801 was a comparatively quiet period for the British as far as effective military action was concerned. Malta was finally captured in 1800 (in the process both *Généreux* and *Guillaume Tell*, the last two French survivors of the Nile, were taken), and remained a British naval base for the next century and a half. The French ships stayed quietly in Brest and Toulon until the spring of 1801.

In the early months of 1801 the Battle of Copenhagen was fought in the Baltic and Tsar Paul I of Russia died. There was comparative calm throughout Europe. Only in Egypt was the war still alive.

The French army, after its retreat from Acre was static in Egypt. A British army under General Abercromby was in the Mediterranean on the way to attack it; Napoleon was making efforts to reinforce it.

While Abercromby was training his troops in seaborne assault on the shores of Asia Minor, Admiral Honoré Ganteaume had escaped with seven ships of the line from Brest. On board he had troops destined for the relief of Egypt and he was sailing for Alexandria. Ganteaume was dogged by ill fortune; he was obliged to put in to Toulon for repairs and, even after this, had to leave three ships, under Admiral Linois, to patch themselves up in Leghorn (now in French hands). His four remaining ships did not reach Alexandria and Ganteaume returned, discouraged, to Toulon. On the way there he did gain a consolation prize in the shape of the capture of *Swiftsure*, 74, which remained in French hands until recaptured at Trafalgar.

By this time, Abercromby and his men had won the battle of Alexandria (in which Abercromby was killed) and the fate of the French in Egypt was sealed. Peace talks were in the air, and Napoleon was anxious that the British delegates should not enter into them having the moral advantage of a recent victory. He made desperate efforts to keep the war in Egypt alive. When Ganteaume failed, Linois, in Leghorn, was given new orders; he was to return to Cadiz, link up with twelve ships there and make another attempt to reach Egypt. Linois was delayed by contrary weather and it was the beginning of July before he had reached Algeciras on his way to Cadiz. By this time, operations in Egypt were finished, and the French army there defeated.

Sir James Saumarez, who had commanded *Orion* at the Nile, was now flag officer in command of the blockade of Cadiz. On learning of Linois's arrival in Algeciras, he sailed, on 6 July, to attack. The attack failed and Saumarez had to withdraw, leaving *Hannibal*, 74, aground and in French hands. There were explanations, in the form of shallows and contrary winds, but it was one of the worst reverses the Royal Navy had suffered. Five days later, both sides having been reinforced from the blockaders or blockaded at Cadiz, a second battle was fought. This ended more satisfactorily for Saumarez, with three Spanish ships destroyed or taken and the survivors bottled up in Cadiz.

A few months later the preliminaries of the Treaty of Amiens were signed and there were eighteen months of uneasy peace. Some of the hardest work and fiercest battles were yet to come.

CHAPTER 10

Trafalgar: Their Last Battle

Trafalgar was not, of course, the last action under sail, but it was the last major battle, in a major war, fought by ships of the line. No earlier battle was quite like it and nothing like it can ever happen again.

It was foreshadowed almost as soon as the shaky peace treaty signed at Amiens in 1802 finally collapsed in May 1803. This time, Britain's entry into the war was not just an incident in the general European upheaval; Britain was now Napoleon's principal enemy. The constant threat of British sea power around the perimeter of French influence remained a flaw in his most brilliant victories. Until this flaw was eliminated, there could be no final stability for the French Empire. Napoleon realised that he could not beat the Royal Navy at sea; but it could be beaten by land. If the supremely successful French army could be landed in England, the navy would be of no more account than the tentacles of a sea monster with its heart destroyed.

The task of Napoleon's army would not be easy; but by organisation and training and with adequate equipment the outcome could be made certain. L'Armée d'Angleterre was formed and preparations began. There was a lot to do. Eighteenth-century armies fought almost in the formal lines in which they drilled; and marched into battle in compact units, every movement controlled by a word of command. A lot of training would be required to accustom men to get quickly and effectively into battle from the confusion of a massed landing from boats in the face of determined opposition. The craft being constructed to convey them across the Channel were described as flat-bottomed but their shape had to be at least minimally seaworthy, which meant that they would touch the ground in some feet of water.

The troops would have to jump into sinister-looking surf and wade ashore like the standard-bearer of the Tenth Legion eighteen hundred and sixty years before.

All these problems could be overcome by training and preparation, and the work went steadily ahead. By the autumn of 1804 Napoleon was ready to tackle the problem of gaining command of the Channel, or at least the Straits of Dover. Theoretically it might have been possible to row the invasion craft across in a period of flat calm, in which the defending ships could not move. In practice this was not a serious possibility. To get the troops out of their camps, into the boats and out of harbour would take a good deal longer than to row across the Straits, and flat calms do not often last long in the Channel. With the first catspaw of wind even a few frigates would make a shambles of the rowing fleet. The French navy had to achieve command of the Straits, even if only for a couple of days. It would not matter if it were then driven away, as the army could live well off the land in the lush Kentish countryside, and, by the time more French supplies were required, would be dictating peace terms in London.

At the end of 1804 the bulk of the French navy was in three main groups. Admiral Villeneuve was in Toulon with some twelve ships of the line; Admiral Missiessy was in Rochefort with five; and Admiral Ganteaume was in Brest with twenty-one. In addition there were a dozen Spanish ships of the line in Ferrol and about half as many in Cadiz. They were being blockaded by Nelson at Toulon, Sir William Cornwallis at Brest and Collingwood at Ferrol. There were six French ships of the line in the West Indies, where the islands previously taken by the British had been handed back after the Treaty of Amiens.

Napoleon's plan for breaking the stalemate, and thwarting the British defence, was majestic in its scale and concept. On occasion he had reproved his generals for 'making pictures', that is, deceiving themselves by seeing things as they would like them to be and not as they actually were. Napoleon was now making a picture – a masterpiece, but a picture all the same. His orders were that Villeneuve, Missiessy and Ganteaume were, at appropriate times, to dodge the blockade and leave port. Villeneuve and Missiessy were to collect what Spanish ships were available, sail to the West Indies, and there create havoc by attacking the British-held islands. This would draw the British fleets away from Europe, whereupon Villeneuve was to leave the West Indies, double back and, joined by Ganteaume, sail straight for the Channel. By this time he should have about forty

French ships of the line and some twenty Spanish; with this fleet he could brush aside any opposition and arrive at the Straits of Dover in force. The invasion army would cross the Straits and all would be over.

The tragic figure of the Trafalgar campaign is Admiral Pierre Villeneuve. Perhaps, if he had been a crazed revolutionary firebrand, he might have been able to consider this plan, in which his was the key role, with enthusiasm – initially at least. Villeneuve, however, was no kind of fanatic; he was a steady, competent man, perfectly willing to fight but very much aware of the massive odds against Napoleon's plan. He knew the limitations of the undertrained French crews, he knew the state of the ships and their lack of adequate maintenance, and he knew that the state of the Spanish navy was even worse. Above all, he was a professional, and he knew how unlikely it was that the British and the weather would play the parts Napoleon's imagination had sketched out for them. He was not a defeatist; these were facts and he was aware of them. Through no fault of his own he had arrived too late to join in the attempt at Ireland in 1796; at the Nile it fell to him to slip ignominiously away; and now he was to lead an enterprise which could end only in disaster.

There was no help for it, he had to go; and on 30 March 1805 Villeneuve left Toulon. He was able to do this because Nelson wanted him to leave. Rather than continue indefinitely sitting outside Toulon, Nelson was anxious for Villeneuve to come out and be defeated. To this end he kept the main body of his fleet well away from Toulon in the hope that the French would venture out, whereupon he could pounce.

Unfortunately, Nelson, having heard no whisper of Napoleon's intentions, was waiting to pounce in the wrong place. The long chase to Egypt after Brueys in 1798 was vivid in his memory, and his thoughts were all of protecting the eastern Mediterranean. His eleven ships of the line were lying off Sardinia, whence he could readily intercept any move towards the east. He was no wiser when his frigates returned from off Toulon, and reported that the French were heading south. This could well have meant that they were intending to pass south of Sardinia – almost straight towards him. It was not until ten days after Villeneuve had passed Gibraltar that Nelson learned he was waiting off Sardinia in vain. Even then he could not know whether Villeneuve was heading for the Channel or the Atlantic. Nevertheless, he set off in pursuit, hoping to find better information soon. This did not happen until 10 May when he put in to Lagos in southern Portugal. There he learned that the French were bound for the West Indies. Nelson set off across the Atlantic; there was no point in remaining on his Mediterranean station – the ships he was supposed to be blockading were no longer there.

Meanwhile, Missiessy had got away from Rochefort, reached the West Indies and, because a vital order did not reach him, left again and returned to Europe, missing both Villeneuve and Nelson. He plays no further part in the story of Trafalgar.

Ganteaume, on the other hand, was unable to break out of Brest. Cornwallis's blockade, following the example of Lord St Vincent, was too close; it could be broken only if the French were prepared to fight their way out. Ganteaume offered to do so but was ordered by Napoleon not to risk his fleet in this way. Unaware that Nelson was about to cross the Atlantic, Napoleon made a new picture, resulting in fresh orders to Villeneuve. He was not to wait for Ganteaume but, as soon as he had created enough havoc in the West Indies, was to return to Europe, collect the Spanish ships from Ferrol, go to Brest, fight off Cornwallis, and release Ganteaume. Then he was to sail up the Channel as originally ordered. The despair felt by Villeneuve as he contemplated this order may be imagined. If, as originally planned, Ganteaume had broken out and the British fleets had been eluded, and if the weather had been right, there might have been a fighting chance of getting up the Channel. Now Villeneuve was required to seek out a battle with the very fleet guarding the Channel, a fleet, moreover, which would most certainly be reinforced at the first hint of a possible attack from outside Brest. It was madness.

Nevertheless, Villeneuve started to obey and made preparations to assault British islands in the Caribbean. Hardly had he given the orders when he was told of Nelson's imminent arrival. There would have been no point whatever in fighting Nelson in the West Indies. In fact, his arrival gave some substance to Napoleon's plans, for at least one British fleet had been lured away from European waters. Villeneuve's obvious move now was to avoid Nelson and get back to Europe. This he did, so far adequately complying with Napoleon's orders. Nelson, as soon as he learned that the French had left, also turned east and sailed back across the Atlantic.

From now on, things began to fall apart for Villeneuve; he had evaded Nelson but was seen in mid-Atlantic by the British brig *Curieux* on her way, with dispatches from Nelson, to the Admiralty in London. Lord Barham, now First Lord, received the news from *Curieux* on 9 July and had time to make plans for Villeneuve's reception. Already all hope of a surprise attack on Cornwallis had gone. Instead, fifteen ships of the line, under Rear-Admiral Sir Robert Calder, were detached from Cornwallis's fleet and sailed to meet him.

Meanwhile, Nelson had reached European waters and, still very conscious of the potential threat to the Mediterranean, made for Gibraltar. He arrived there on 19 July, when Villeneuve was still far out in the Atlantic. Learning that the French had not returned, he realised at once that if the threat was not to the Mediterranean, it could well be to the Channel. In such a situation, and in the absence of more precise information, there was only one course open to a British admiral – look to the Western Approaches. Nelson sailed north to join Cornwallis. On 22 July Villeneuve encountered Calder.

Robert Calder was another admiral unblessed by fortune. When he met the French fleet the weather was misty and the wind was light: not easy conditions in which to fight a decisive battle. Calder was a conventional man, slow to accept new ways. He had been Sir John Jervis's flag captain at Cape St Vincent, and had not approved of Nelson leaving the line of battle, even though victory was assured thereby. In the conditions in which he met the French fleet, conventional methods almost guaranteed an indecisive result. Flair and imagination were called for, and these Calder did not possess. If he had ordered his ships to go straight for the French, each one as best it could, something might have been achieved. Instead he ordered the line to tack in succession so as to come up to the enemy in formation and in an orderly manner. The wind was light and the visibility was poor and there was simply not time for this manoeuvre to work properly. Consequently, although two ships were taken, the main body of the French got away unscathed.

Villeneuve's orders envisaged his lying off Ferrol for a short period, while the Spanish ships in the harbour came out to join him, and then sweeping on to Brest. Harsh reality required him to get into port as soon as he could. Instead of becoming fine-tuned by the double crossing of the Atlantic, his ships were in need of repair and his men were in need of rest. He made for the nearest port, Vigo, and perhaps for a while felt relieved to get in. His impossible orders, however, would not go away, and soon afterwards he sailed for Ferrol where he joined the twelve Spanish ships of the line. On 13 August he sailed out of Ferrol with his combined fleet.

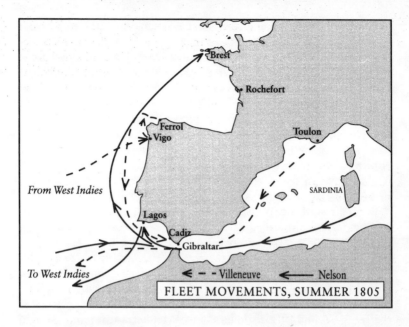

Brest

Rochefort

Ferrol
Vigo

Toulon

From West Indies

SARDINIA

Lagos

Cadiz
Gibraltar

To West Indies

← - - Villeneuve   ← — Nelson

FLEET MOVEMENTS, SUMMER 1805

Villeneuve now had a total of about thirty ships of the line, in which he had no confidence. His orders required him to seek battle with the twenty or so ships of Cornwallis's fleet, plus Nelson's eleven, plus whatever reinforcements had been sent from Channel ports since Calder reported back three weeks before. Each of the British ships had been continuously at sea except for regular visits to well-equipped dockyards; their crews had been drilled by experts. His own fleet had been long in harbour, without adequate dockyard support, until the sudden transatlantic crossings, which had shown up weaknesses he had not the resources to correct. His crews had had their skills (although not, as they later proved, their courage) rotted by years in port. It would have been better for Villeneuve personally if he had taken his fleet straight into battle, regardless of the consequences. Had he considered only his own desperate position he might well have done so; but when it came to the crunch he was too responsible a man, and perhaps too good a senior officer, deliberately to squander his men's lives and his country's ships in a battle which could not be won. He sailed out of Ferrol but, instead of turning north towards Cornwallis, turned south to Cadiz. Waiting outside Cadiz was Collingwood, who kept clear as the combined fleet sailed in and then resumed the blockade, like a shepherd closing the pen at the end of a sheepdog trial.

There, for a while, the matter rested. Meanwhile a momentous event, of which Villeneuve had not been told, had taken place. Napoleon, before he received news of Villeneuve's retreat, had called off the invasion. While the Armée d'Angleterre waited at Boulogne for naval supremacy, trouble had been brewing in central Europe. Russia and Austria had formed a new coalition against Napoleon and their troops were massing; it was a threat which could not be ignored. The Armée d'Angleterre had its name changed to the Grande Armée and it was marched away from the Channel towards Austerlitz, Jena, Friedland, the treaty of Tilsit and, at the end, the snows of Russia.

For the rest of the summer of 1805 an uneasy lull prevailed at sea. Villeneuve was blockaded in Cadiz by Collingwood, who was being steadily reinforced. Nelson in *Victory* returned to England to report and take some leave at his home in Merton, Surrey, where he considered his tactics for the forthcoming battle. Everyone knew there would have to be a battle and that it would be fought by Nelson. Villeneuve's fleet was an enlargement of the Toulon fleet which was the responsibility of Nelson as C-in-C Mediterranean; and it could not stay in Cadiz indefinitely. There were not enough resources in Cadiz to sustain a fleet of more than thirty sail of the line for a lengthy period. Any stores from France had to travel in creaking ox wagons over 900 miles of appalling roads, and Spanish resources were meagre.

There was no relief for Villeneuve. He had not yet heard Napoleon's accusation of cowardice but he knew that such an accusation would be made. In fact, there were whispers to the same effect amongst his own fleet. His relations with his ally were uneasy; the French were far from popular with the Spanish, who were reluctant to supply desperately needed goods and services. He did not know what his next move was going to be and, outside the harbour entrance, the British fleet built up like a scaffold being erected outside the condemned cell. On top of everything, he had an enemy in his own flagship in the shape of General Alexandre Lauriston, the commander of the troops with the fleet. Lauriston was an honorary ADC to Napoleon and, as such, was allowed to correspond with him direct. He employed this privilege to traduce and vilify Villeneuve in every way that ignorance of the sea and meanness of spirit could suggest. So far from disciplining Lauriston, Napoleon accepted everything he had to say. Dislike and distrust of Villeneuve, for failing to achieve the impossible, built up in the emperor's mind and must have affected his subsequent decisions.

On 12 September, Nelson left Portsmouth for the last time and, on the 28th, arrived off Cadiz. His coming had been eagerly awaited by the fleet, which had been under the command of Vice-Admiral Cuthbert Collingwood for some weeks. To his wife and family Collingwood was a loving husband and devoted father, but this aspect of himself he kept solely to his family. To his subordinates he was efficient and just, but totally unresponsive. He and Nelson had been friends for many years but, apart from their common professional background, their characters were very different. Collingwood was a good, steady man and a good commander; Nelson was a volatile man and a superlative commander. Just as the news that Wellington would be in command was greeted with enthusiasm by the army before Waterloo, so the arrival of Nelson was greeted with joy before Trafalgar. Both had the gift which is beyond competence, beyond even brilliance, which creates instant confidence and *esprit de corps*. Certainly after Nelson's arrival, morale outside Cadiz was high.

On 9 October, Nelson produced a memorandum which was to be circulated to the captains in the fleet, and in which he set out the results of his deliberations at Merton. His previous battles had been special cases, in which his approach was to a large extent dictated by the position the enemy had taken up; now it would be two fleets in the open sea, and the method of attack was entirely up to him. The memorandum makes it clear that an attack in one long line of battle would not be practicable; a day would not be long enough for all ships to get into action and the result would be indecisive. Instead he stated his intention of attacking in two lines or groups, one to head for the centre of the enemy's line, the other to attack near the rear. The enemy ships not attacked (the van, or about the first quarter of the enemy line) would initially continue on course. It would take time for the commander of the enemy's van to be sure of what was happening, and it would take time to turn his ships round while maintaining some sort of order. Consequently, it was very probable that the centre and rear would be overwhelmed by superior numbers before the van could get back to help. Depending on the direction of the wind, it might be very difficult for the van to get back at all. This then, was the 'Nelson touch'; far from the traditional concept of fighting in orderly lines of battle, there was to be a headlong assault from the flank. The centre and rear were to be destroyed quickly; the van could be dealt with later.

It is possible, when giving orders, to make them very precise. As things never go exactly as anticipated the commander then has the option, should things go wrong, of complaining that his orders were not properly carried out. Nelson scorned to do this. Having set out his intentions in some detail, his memorandum said:

> But in case signals can neither be seen nor perfectly understood, no captain can do very wrong if he places his ship alongside that of an enemy.

This was sublime. One of the worst states an officer can be in is to be surrounded by the confusion of battle and unsure of what he ought to do. Nelson's captains were spared this. They were given a straightforward instruction to be followed if in any doubt; and, by implication, they were to be fighting under a leader who, so long as they did their best, would support them. They would not, afterwards, be accused of not sticking to some complicated plan by someone trying to cover up his mistakes.

The British fleet was confident and ready for anything. Villeneuve, in Cadiz harbour, had a new problem. He had received fresh instructions. Napoleon, now absorbed in a campaign in Austria, ordered him to leave port at the first opportunity and sail to Naples where he was to land the 4,000 troops he had with the fleet. The intention was that the extra troops in southern Italy would discourage any action by British forces stationed in Malta and Sicily; but in the nature of things it was a vague and impracticable scheme. The chance of getting away unscathed from Nelson was small, and if this were achieved, it could take anything from ten days to a month to get to Naples, depending on the weather. It is hard to believe that Napoleon's strategy depended very heavily on so uncertain a proceeding. Yet, for it, he was prepared to risk the possible loss of thirty ships of the line. It says a lot about Napoleon's attitude to his navy.

Villeneuve's problem was that the Spaniards were unwilling to move. They had many objections, but what they all amounted to was that they knew all too well the odds against them. The Spanish navy, even more than the French, was suffering from lack of proper support and attention; furthermore their alliance with France had been forced on them, and they had no burning desire to go to their destruction for the greater glory of Napoleon. Villeneuve had to resort to a council of war – that prelude to failure – in an attempt to achieve agreement. The council's decision was that it would not be practicable to sail unless Nelson divided his fleet; with that Villeneuve had to be content for the moment.

Fate dealt Villeneuve one more blow; he heard that he was to be replaced. Napoleon, almost it seems as an afterthought, had decided to inflict this punishment upon him and Admiral Rosily was sent to Cadiz with Villeneuve's dismissal in his pocket. No direct word was sent to Villeneuve; he picked up the news from rumours. It is possible that Decrès, the minister responsible, sympathising with Villeneuve, had deliberately held back a direct order to give him the chance of doing something before Rosily arrived. Certainly Villeneuve interpreted the absence of a direct order as meaning that he was free to go, if the opportunity arose, before Rosily's arrival. He realised that the one hope he had of salvaging his career would be to command a successful operation. One thing was certain: the fleet would go whether he was in command of it or not, so the possibility of conserving the lives of his men and his ships did not arise. To go, he would have to get the Spaniards to move; the opportunity to do so came when he received a report that Nelson had sent five ships to Gibraltar and Tetuan to replenish stores. This could be described as dividing his fleet and the council of war's stipulation was met. Villeneuve ordered the combined fleet to sea.

The departure from Cadiz began on 19 October. Conditions were far from ideal. The wind was light and westerly which meant that the ships could barely keep a course to clear the harbour entrance, and, once outside, had barely enough way to keep clear of the rocky shore to leeward. Only a few ships had got away by nightfall. At dawn on the 20th, the wind backed to SSW, which made it easier to leave Cadiz, but once outside the best course which could be made good was about due west – out into the Atlantic. However, at about 4 p.m. the wind veered again to the west, enabling Villeneuve to turn to the south-east, his course for the Straits of Gibraltar.

All this was observed by the British frigates and reported to Nelson who was lying with his ships of the line about fifty miles to the west. He did not want to discourage Villeneuve from coming out by maintaining too obvious a presence. Villeneuve had one small chance of getting clear away, and that depended on exceptionally good

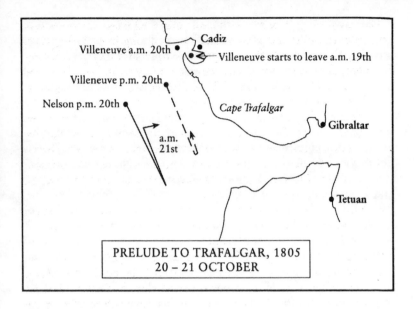

PRELUDE TO TRAFALGAR, 1805
20 – 21 OCTOBER

fortune with the weather. If, once the whole fleet were out, the wind increased to near gale force westerly, he could run for the straits, and Nelson would not be able to do a great deal to stop him. Battles could not be fought in strong winds. It was too dangerous for ships to lie close to each other, and at longer range any accurate gunnery was impossible. In fact, in really rough seas, any gunnery at all was impossible because the guns would be unmanageable on violently heaving decks. A gale did come, but two days too late for Villeneuve.

On learning that Villeneuve was starting to come out, Nelson sailed for the mouth of the straits. On reaching there on the morning of the 20th, he learned that the combined fleet was still barely out of Cadiz harbour, and would not reach the straits that day. He therefore sailed west and north, and by evening was about fifteen miles south-west of Villeneuve, out of sight, but constantly informed by his frigates.

Throughout the night of the 20–21 October, the two fleets were sailing on roughly parallel courses towards the south-east. They were invisible to each other, but not to Nelson's frigates under Captain Henry Blackwood, which were sailing between the fleets and regularly reporting the French position to *Victory*. At about 4 a.m. on the 21st, Nelson wore round, and sailed NNE to intercept.

The dawn of 21 October 1805 was grey and hazy; the wind was light from the west and a great swell was coming in with the wind, heralding the storm which was approaching. As the day grew lighter the enemy fleet was seen about ten miles away to the east, and the final run in to the battle began. The early approach was made almost in silence, maximum speed was about 2–2½ knots, the only sounds the occasional flap of a sail as a ship pitched and a surge of water as bows plunged into the troughs of the swell. At about 7 a.m. *Victory* flew the signals requiring the fleet to form two lines, prepare for battle and bear up to the east; this was the move envisaged in Nelson's memorandum. The fleet turned to starboard and, in battle formation, steered for the enemy.

At 8 a.m. Villeneuve ordered his fleet to wear round and head back to the north-west. His move was not prompted by any hope of avoiding action; it was, most certainly, too late for that. But by turning round he turned away from the comparatively open waters of the straits, which were by now close at hand. In a battle in open water there would be a tendency for hard-pressed ships to drift downwind and become scattered. On his new course his ships had nowhere to go downwind except the rocky coast and the headland of Cape Trafalgar standing out to starboard. This was a powerful incentive for ships' captains to keep as far as possible to windward, facing the uncertain risks of battle rather than certain destruction on the coast. It took the unskilled French and Spaniards some time to execute the manoeuvre of wearing, but they did it, and not too badly. The new line settled down and watched the British running down towards them, not in silence now but with bands playing and crews cheering.

Nelson, in *Victory*, led the larboard line or column and Collingwood in *Royal Sovereign* the starboard line. The wind was roughly west and the two columns were heading about ENE so that, although both were running with the wind, Nelson's was, marginally, the windward division and Collingwood's the leeward. Because of the relative dispositions of the two fleets when the lines had been formed, *Royal Sovereign* was nearer to the enemy than *Victory* and would be the first ship into action.

A feature of the approach which caused some comment and discussion in after years was that Nelson's division was more or less in line ahead, whereas Collingwood ordered his ships to form a line of bearing, that is, to approach in line abreast. In neither division was there much formal order – each ship was sailing into battle as fast as it could; but Collingwood's division was more spread out than Nelson's. In theory, by approaching in line abreast, as was attempted on the First of June and at Camperdown, each ship would begin action simultaneously. In practice, this did not happen. It would have involved faster ships slowing down to allow slower ships to catch up and keep in line. Battle conditions usually precluded such precision. Nevertheless, in any formation resembling line abreast, each ship would receive broadsides as she approached. As Nelson did it, *Victory* took most of the punishment; the lighter 74s astern of her were largely shielded. Any enemy ship not directly athwart Nelson's line of approach had to fire her guns obliquely to hit anyone in the approaching column; and the angle at which the guns were trained changed constantly. In these circumstances, there was little hope of any accuracy; only a ship which had *Victory* directly abeam could fire broadsides at any fast rate of fire. So *Victory* took the brunt of it. Discussion of the merits of the two forms of approach is largely academic since, in both divisions, ships scrambled into battle as fast as they could, and there was no question of anybody reducing sail to allow slower ships to keep in any kind of order.

At about half past eleven Nelson made his immortal signal, 'England expects that every man will do his duty.' It was received with cheers. Cheering was a common form of expression in the navy; sometimes it was a spontaneous display of excitement or approval by the crews, and sometimes they were ordered to cheer as part of an exchange of courtesies or to intimidate the enemy. On this occasion the cheers were probably of the latter kind, since all comments recorded were to the effect that the signal was a bit superfluous; everybody had every intention of doing his duty. But Nelson had a great sense of occasion; that signal, made at that time, has been adequately approved by posterity. There were only two more signals. The first was to prepare to anchor, indicating Nelson's intention to anchor at the end of the day. The second was that always flown in battle – almost as much a battle cry as a signal: 'Engage the enemy more closely.'

As the two fleets drew closer, most men were thinking of their wives and homes. In his cabin, Nelson was amending his will, in an attempt to have official provision made for Lady Hamilton (which officialdom ignored – she died in poverty), and writing his famous prayer for a 'great and glorious victory'. Nelson was a man with many personal faults, but nothing can take from him his inspiration and vision. 'May no misconduct in anyone tarnish it; and may humanity after Victory be the dominant feature in the British Fleet' must be as noble a sentiment as any expressed by any military leader.

Villeneuve, on *Bucentaure*, knew what was coming. Long before the battle he had forecast that Nelson would attack his centre and rear. At the Nile, Nelson had attacked the French van and centre, and Villeneuve, then in the rear, had been very conscious of the difficulty of moving forward to their help. The comparable tactic with fleets under way was to attack the centre and rear, when it would be difficult for the van to turn and get back to help. Villeneuve had the prescience to foresee this but, with light winds and lack of expertise, there was little he could do about it. He could only wait and, with an aptness not often displayed by events, *Victory* steered straight for *Bucentaure*.

At about midday the long period of fleet movements and counter movements, and the ordeal of the slow approach to battle came to an end. *Royal Sovereign* drove into the enemy line and rounded up on the leeside of the Spanish first-rate *Santa Ana*, flagship of Vice-Admiral d'Alava. Within a few minutes, *Victory* was in close action. Nelson had headed for the stern of *Bucentaure* and, as *Victory* approached, *Redoutable* next astern to *Bucentaure* pressed forward so as to leave no gap between them. Captain Hardy pointed out that he was bound to hit one of them; 'It doesn't signify,' said Nelson. 'Take your choice.' *Victory*'s wheel had already been smashed and she was being controlled by the massive tiller on her lower gundeck. The order was given and she scraped past the stern of *Bucentaure*, each gun of the larboard broadside pumping shot into her as it passed, and crashed into the larboard bow of *Redoutable*.

Captain Lucas of *Redoutable* was a man of fiery temperament and much energy, who had great faith in small-arms fire and boarding tactics; what is more, in spite of the long, morale-sapping periods in harbour, he had thoroughly trained his crew. As the bows of the two ships ground together, grappling irons were thrown aboard *Victory* and a boarding party assembled on *Redoutable*. While *Victory*'s guns hammered *Redoutable* below decks, Lucas maintained a withering small-arms fire on *Victory*'s quarterdeck in preparation for boarding. So fierce was the fire that Hardy ordered all men on the quarterdeck who could to take cover, an unusual action in those days. Of course, admirals could not be seen to take cover from anything and Nelson continued to walk the quarterdeck in the gold-laced, order-studded

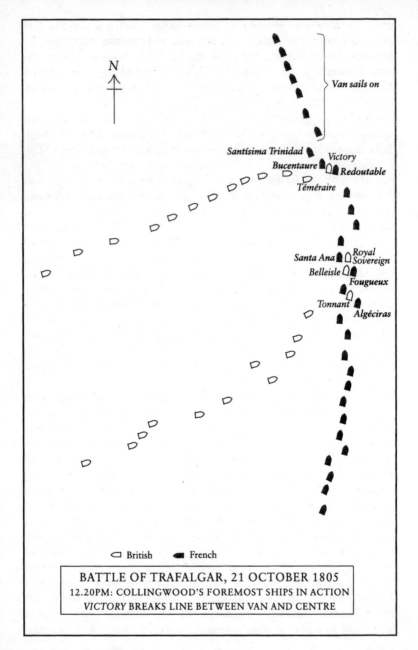

N

Van sails on

Santísima Trinidad
Bucentaure *Victory*
Redoutable
Téméraire

Santa Ana *Royal Sovereign*
Belleisle
Fougueux
Tonnant
Algéciras

British   French

BATTLE OF TRAFALGAR, 21 OCTOBER 1805
12.20PM: COLLINGWOOD'S FOREMOST SHIPS IN ACTION
VICTORY BREAKS LINE BETWEEN VAN AND CENTRE

coat which he had refused to remove and which proclaimed him as a very important target. An attempt at boarding was made by *Redoutable* which was repulsed by *Victory*'s Marines. Then the almost inevitable happened and Nelson received his fatal wound. The admiral of the fleet which was to wreak such destruction with its big guns was mortally wounded by a musket shot.

Victory's guns were steadily in action with *Redoutable* to starboard and, at intervals, with *Bucentaure* to larboard. *Bucentaure* was soon forced to surrender; several ships had followed through the gap in the French line made by *Victory* and each one as she passed fired her larboard broadside into the helpless stern of *Bucentaure*, causing desperate damage throughout her length. All her boats were shattered, and Villeneuve was unable to transfer his flag to another ship; he was taken prisoner. *Victory* was severely damaged in the exchanges, but she was soon relieved by *Téméraire* which came up on the starboard side of *Redoutable*. For a while Lucas, in his two-decker, was fighting two first-rates, and he was obliged to strike after very heavy losses.

The situation of *Victory* was typical of the whole battle. Many ships were in yardarm-to-yardarm combat with their adversaries and many, both British and French, found themselves in simultaneous action with opponents to both starboard and larboard. Several pairs fought each other to a standstill like *Belleisle* and *Fougueux*, *Tonnant* and *Algéciras* or *Royal Sovereign* and *Santa Ana*. Many ships on both sides sustained great damage.

The French and Spanish ships which fought well faced greater odds than they should have because of the conduct of a few ships, in particular those in the van. It was obviously difficult for the ships ahead of Villeneuve, especially in the light wind, to turn about and get back to the battle in a short time – which Nelson had relied on in his plan. But they took longer than they should have done. Villeneuve signalled to the van to support him but *Bucentaure*'s masts were toppling and wreathed in smoke and the signal was not seen. In command of the van was Admiral Dumanoir. He had seven ships and, with them, he continued sailing north after the battle started. He may not have seen the signal recalling him, but it took an unnecessarily long time for him to decide that his proper course was to support his commander-in-chief. When he did turn round, he headed not for the thick of the battle but, keeping well to seaward, towards the rear. His intention, he said later, was to cut off those British ships not yet fully engaged. The wind had become even lighter and there were, indeed, a few British ships which, being slow sailers and well behind the leaders at the start, were still slowly approaching the battle. It was, at best, a rather pedestrian course to take and it achieved nothing. After a brief exchange of shots in which Dumanoir's ship, *Formidable*, was damaged by raking broadsides, he continued with three other ships, to the south and out of the picture. Two of his Spanish ships headed for Cadiz, but one of Dumanoir's captains was made of sterner stuff. Captain Infernet of *Intrépide*, once allowed to turn about, ignored Dumanoir and made for the centre of the battle. *Intrépide* was the last ship to strike after her masts fell and with her rudder out of action. Infernet survived as, it is pleasing to record, did his ten-year-old son who was with him.

In addition to the half-dozen ships in the van which were slow to get into action, there were a few others in the centre or the rear which turned away in the face of the British onslaught and did not make adequate effort to get back into battle. They exchanged only a few shots before making for Cadiz. Out of Villeneuve's thirty-three ships, about ten either did not fight or took an ineffective part. Although Villeneuve had the larger fleet, and those that did fight did so with matchless courage, he was, for practical purposes, outnumbered.

Great courage and determination were shown by both sides, but the battle was won by superior gunnery. The British could maintain much the faster rate of fire and enemy casualties mounted much faster than their own. It is difficult to be precise about French and Spanish casualties in the battle, because so many were lost afterwards in the storm, but eighteen French and Spanish ships each had between 200 and 550 killed or wounded. Only one British ship, *Colossus*, had 200 casualties, three others, of which *Victory* was one, had between 100 and 160. No amount of courage could outweigh this sort of imbalance. When a ship suffered casualties to the extent that so many French and Spanish ships did, it was not a question of giving in; it was impossible to continue, and the only option left to her captain was surrender. A total of sixteen ships were taken on 21 October, another blew up and one retired so damaged that she later ran ashore.

The log of *Victory* says, 'Partial firing continued until 4.30 when, a victory having been reported to the Right Hon. Lord Viscount Nelson, K.B., and Commander-in-Chief, he then died of his wounds.' Command of the fleet passed to Collingwood.

It was a grim moment to achieve high command; Collingwood now had to cope with the sixteen prizes and the many badly damaged

British ships, and a storm was coming. Nelson had made it clear that he intended to anchor after the battle, and had again urged it upon Captain Hardy as he lay dying. Collingwood clearly did not agree and made no attempt to anchor when he had taken command. Whether he should have done so and whether it would have prevented some of the disasters which were to follow, no one can now say. Collingwood was the man on the spot and had to act on his own judgement. He had plenty to think about. There had been a general drift towards the shore during the battle, the wind was rising, almost all ships – victors and vanquished – were damaged and many were crippled. Ships with their masts and rigging destroyed had to be taken in tow by those which could set some amount of sail.

The prizes, in particular, were at considerable risk; all were severely damaged and all had prisoners, including many wounded, secured below decks. The British ships with their own vital repairs to masts and rigging to see to, could spare only minimum numbers for prize crews. A small prize crew could manage in calm conditions but a storm was coming. Its onset would change everything, but meanwhile things were cobbled together, and the fleet began to tow its damaged ships and its prizes away from the dangerous coast.

Towing to windward was always desperately slow. A ship of the line could barely claw herself away from a lee shore in heavy weather; with an ungainly hulk in tow she would be fortunate if she were able merely to hold her position and counter the drift towards the shore. Throughout the night of the 21–22 October, the wind continued to increase and by noon on the 22nd, it was approaching gale force; many ships found that a tow could not be sustained. When it became apparent that a tow must be abandoned, it was not just a matter of cutting the cable; before that could be thought of, the men on the tow had to be transferred. There were the British prize crews, the French wounded and the prisoners. The prisoners might be expected to co-operate with their rescuers, but the language difficulty would still make them very difficult to control in the wild conditions of heaving decks, heavy rain and wind. Many ships' boats had been damaged or lost, making the process of transfer slower still. At first, it was a matter of taking men off before prizes were deliberately abandoned; as the gale continued, tows began to break away, and it became a question of saving whoever could be saved before the tow drifted away out of practicable reach.

In general, Nelson's prayer for humanity in victory was answered;

herculean efforts were made, but the lot of the wounded was truly dreadful. There was no gentle way of moving a helpless man from below decks in a shattered hulk up damaged – if indeed existing – ladders to an open deck, lowering him into a wildly tossing small boat and then repeating the process in reverse. Some suffered tortures and lived, many died, and many could not be rescued in time. A number of ships drove ashore. When this happened, an active man might just have a chance of getting ashore alive; the wounded had no chance at all.

There were some incidents more cheerful to contemplate; Captain Moorson of *Revenge* told of a prisoner, picked up from the shattered *Achille*, who turned out to be a woman. She was one of the small band of heroines in history who managed, against all odds, to join a service disguised as men, in order to be near their husbands. She was picked up by the cutter *Pickle* and transferred to *Revenge*, where she was courteously treated, and clothes were made for her. Among the prisoners who were already aboard *Revenge* she found her husband. It is to be hoped that they both survived to return, at last, to normal domestic life.

Three ships were retaken by prisoners. They had broken loose and were drifting and the prize crews were too few in number to clear decks, tangled with fallen rigging, and try to get some control under jury rig. If the prisoners were released, they might be able to achieve something. It was a choice between drifting on to the rocks in British hands or perhaps, just possibly, getting into Cadiz harbour in French or Spanish hands. The transfers were effected without bloodshed, and all nationalities worked together against their common enemy, the sea. *Bucentaure* changed hands in this manner and reached the harbour entrance before grounding; those aboard were saved. *Algéciras* successfully entered harbour. *Santa Ana* managed to keep afloat until the afternoon of the 23rd, when a sortie was made by ships in the harbour to tow her in.

Altogether, sixteen French and Spanish ships were taken on the day of the battle; two more escaped capture but were destroyed, *Achille* by explosion and *Indomptable* by running ashore some days later. Dumanoir, and the four ships which sailed south away from the battle, were captured by Admiral Sir Richard Strachan the following month. The fortunes of the combined fleet may be summarised as follows:

Taken in battle and in due course towed to Gibraltar	4
Taken in battle but subsequently lost in gale (including *Bucentaure*, retaken by French but subsequently lost)	10
Destroyed on day of battle or by wreck soon afterwards	2
Escaped but foundered subsequently in Cadiz	2
Captured subsequently by Admiral Strachan	4
	22
Taken in battle, retaken in gale and survived	2
Escaped from battle to Cadiz	9
	11

Thus, the total number of French or Spanish ships taken or destroyed at, or as a direct result of, Trafalgar was twenty-two leaving eleven ships in Cadiz. For practical purposes, there they remained. Within three years, Spain became Britain's ally and in that period no major French or Spanish enterprise was attempted.

After six days of struggle, when all but four of the prizes had been lost or abandoned, and all who could be had been rescued, Collingwood sent a message, under a flag of truce, offering to return the wounded to Cadiz. The offer was accepted and a number of courtesies were exchanged, including the return of prize crews who had fallen into Spanish hands.

Thereafter the British fleet was able to limp slowly back to Gibraltar, and Trafalgar was over. Of those who survived and eventually returned to their peacetime lives, there is no ready record. Of the leaders, Nelson died at the moment of victory and remains for ever a hero. Collingwood became C-in-C Mediterranean and over the next five years wrecked his health grappling with its many complex problems – he died on the voyage home when he was finally relieved in 1810. Villeneuve was taken back to England but was quite soon released and allowed to return to France. There he died in a hotel bedroom at Rennes, apparently by suicide but possibly murdered by government agents.

Trafalgar did not bring peace, as those who fought in it, from Nelson downwards, hoped it might. It did inflict a permanently crippling blow to French naval power, it disposed of all possibility of invasion for the rest of the war, and it settled the pattern of supremacy on the world's oceans for the next hundred years.

CHAPTER 11

After Trafalgar

The great significance and drama of Trafalgar might give the impression that everything that happened afterwards was an anticlimax. This was most certainly not the case. There were indeed differences between the situations before and after; for those thinking of long-term strategy the balance of sea power was materially altered by the battle. But to the men on the ships the differences would not have been very obvious. If they were serving on a ship of the line, it was now less likely that they would be involved in a major sea battle, but they could not know that. Smaller actions were still possible and small actions could be just as lethal as great ones.

The next action came within a fortnight, almost as a postscript to Trafalgar. Vice-Admiral Allemand had taken over the Rochefort squadron from Missiessy, and had been at sea since August, miraculously avoiding detection by the British. The loss of a frigate taking him orders had prevented him joining Villeneuve before Trafalgar, and he was still at sea in November 1805, with Sir Richard Strachan and a squadron from the Brest blockading fleet searching for him. Heading north from Cape Finisterre, was Admiral Dumanoir with the four ships which had sailed out of the battle at Trafalgar; he was hoping to reach a French port, instead of which, on 4 November, he met Strachan. There was poetic justice in this. Allemand was a vigorous and resourceful officer; had he been at the battle, his ships would not have sailed away. Now he remained at large and Dumanoir, with his four fugitive ships, was taken. All the French ships which had been at Trafalgar were now taken, destroyed, or bottled up in Cadiz.

Cadiz was closely blockaded by the Mediterranean Fleet, now under the command of Lord Collingwood. There was a modification to the extent and nature of blockading after the battle. While the threat represented by Villeneuve, Ganteaume, and the Armée d'Angleterre still existed, all other naval tasks had to be subordinated to the vital one of containing the fleets in Brest and Cadiz. Now Villeneuve's fleet was finished, the Armée d'Angleterre had marched away, and Ganteaume's fleet in Brest was not, on its own, a very great menace. Consequently the ships which formed the fleets of Cornwallis and Nelson were largely dispersed to other duties, of which there were many. For example, French privateers were still active, and a menace to British sea trade. They had to be kept in check not only by naval protection of convoys, but by frequent patrols, to keep the narrow seas hostile to them and restrict their movements. This duty could be neglected for a short while, in the face of a compelling emergency, but not indefinitely. Consequently, the number of ships on blockade duty had to be reduced, and a less effective blockade accepted.

Cadiz, however, was to remain a major problem for Collingwood. He had a minimum number of ships with which to carry out the duties of the Mediterranean fleet, and they were usually dispersed far and wide. Unlike at Brest, where reinforcements from the channel ports could soon be provided, Collingwood had only his own resources to rely on, and Cadiz was a potential danger. If the remnants of Villeneuve's fleet were pulled together by some resourceful admiral, they could, if they broke out, become a serious menace to Collingwood's scattered ships. He had, therefore, to perform the near impossible feat of dispersing his ships about the Mediterranean, and at the same time keeping Cadiz under close blockade.

In addition to those in Cadiz, there were about six Spanish ships of the line in Cartagena and some French ships still in Toulon. From any of these places a new threat to the British garrisons in Sicily and Malta could develop. Sicily and, therefore, Malta were already in considerable danger; Napoleon's new campaign against Austria had resulted in the occupation of the whole of mainland Italy, and the British garrison of Sicily faced the French army a mile or so away across the Messina Strait. A new thrust by Napoleon, towards the East, was always a lively possibility and the eastern Mediterranean was now largely controlled by Russia. Russia was to remain Britain's ally until the Treaty of Tilsit in 1807 but her weakness was beginning to be evident. All these considerations made hard work and unremitting anxiety for Collingwood. There was no glory to be won; the most he could hope for was to avoid disaster. The stress of it all eventually destroyed him. There were, however, moments of action, which brought the relief of an occasional success.

At the end of 1805, Collingwood moved most of his fleet into the Mediterranean; Rear-Admiral Louis, with four ships of the line, was left to watch Cadiz. In December, Vice-Admiral Duckworth arrived with reinforcements from England. Pending further orders from Collingwood, Duckworth took command at Cadiz and for a while there was an adequate blockading force there. Meanwhile, taking advantage of the less intensive watch on Brest, two French squadrons from that port got out and away.

One of the squadrons, under Rear-Admiral Willaumez, sailed for the South Atlantic, to attack trading convoys from the East Indies and South America. It got clear away but suffered from foul weather and, before long, returned to Brest having achieved nothing. The other, under Rear-Admiral Leissègues made for the West Indies. Word of their passing Madeira was sent to Duckworth at Cadiz. It was indicative of the buoyant spirit now permeating the navy that he did not hesitate; he sent word to Collingwood and set off in pursuit, leaving one ship of the line to watch Cadiz. At Madeira Duckworth learned that Leissègues' squadron had set off across the Atlantic and, possibly remembering Nelson, he followed. Meanwhile Collingwood, juggling ships and duties, sent two more ships to watch Cadiz. On 6 February 1806 Leissègues and his five ships were caught by Duckworth in Occa Bay, San Domingo (now the Dominican Republic); all five were driven ashore or destroyed.

In the same period, events were stirring in the South Atlantic, unconnected with Willaumez who missed everything. A lone French ship of the line, the 80-gun *Marengo*, with Admiral Linois aboard, had been in the Indian Ocean to augment the overstretched French naval force there. *Marengo* had had some success against East Indiamen too large to be attacked, with confidence, by a frigate on her own. Now she was worn and in need of dockyard repairs, and her crew was diluted by hotch-potch replacements from the East. She had narrowly escaped capture in August 1805 when she met Vice-Admiral Thomas Troubridge on his way to take command of the East Indies station; it was time for her to go home. Linois accordingly retired to the Cape of Good Hope (returned to Holland by the Treaty of Amiens).

He had not been at the Cape long, when Commodore Home

Popham and General Sir David Baird arrived to re-occupy it. Linois had little option but to make his escape and head for France. He did not have the luck of Willaumez or Allemand, and on 13 March 1806 he fell in with the squadron under Sir Borlase Warren, still looking for Willaumez. *Marengo* put up a desperate resistance against impossible odds but inevitably she was taken.

Meanwhile, Rear-Admiral Sir Sidney Smith was on his way to the Mediterranean in the 80-gun *Pompée*. His enterprise and general panache were now generally recognised, but his independent outlook was still regarded with suspicion by senior officers of a conventional turn of mind. Collingwood was among these but, after Acre, he had to admit that Sir Sidney had a flair for inshore operations. Smith was therefore appointed to command the waters around Sicily and southern Italy.

Naples, and Calabria in the south, had been occupied by the French as part of Napoleon's victorious campaign, for which he had abandoned the invasion of England. Only one fortress, at Gaeta, forty-five miles north-west of Naples, still held out. The King of Naples and his court were at Palermo, in Sicily, where there was a substantial British garrison under Major-General Sir John Stuart. Sidney Smith embarked on his new responsibilities with enthusiasm; he first saw to the reinforcement of Gaeta and then captured Capri. This was only a start; in June 1806, supported by the King of Naples, he persuaded General Stuart to make a landing in Calabria, to back up local partisans and to discourage any French build-up against Sicily. Nearly 5,000 men went ashore and, as a large-scale raid, the operation was a definite success. It led to the battle of Maida, in which a larger French attacking force was repulsed by the disciplined musketry of the British infantry. In the resulting euphoria, Smith was made Viceroy of Calabria by the King of Naples.

There was no follow-up and the British troops returned to Sicily. Nothing concrete was achieved, and Rear-Admiral Smith was frowned upon for accepting an unauthorised viceroyship, when he should have been completing his monthly returns to the C-in-C. Nevertheless, it was the first time for five years that British troops had met the French successfully, and the effect on morale was considerable. For one thing, it convinced the future Duke of Wellington that Napoleon's armies were not invincible, if confronted by steady troops; this conviction later encouraged him to embark on his campaigns in Spain.

Meanwhile, Commodore Home Popham and General Sir David Baird had completed the re-occupation of the Cape of Good Hope. Flushed with success, they crossed the South Atlantic and occupied Buenos Aires, at that time a Spanish colony. This was little more than an exuberant gesture, which was not approved by the British government. Buenos Aires was of no strategic value, and not worth the naval and military effort which would have been required to hold it. It was subsequently retaken by Spain, with an ease which would have been even more humiliating than it was, had the loss of Buenos Aires by Britain been of any importance.

In January 1807 the 90-gun *Blenheim*, which had fought at Cape St Vincent, and was long overdue for major repairs, foundered in a storm off Madagascar, on her way home from the East Indies. All hands were lost, including Admiral Troubridge, once the friend of Nelson, one of the original 'band of brothers', and one of the most respected seamen of his time.

1807 was not a good year for the Royal Navy. Following the loss of *Blenheim* and Troubridge came an action in the Dardanelles which ended in failure. The French were showing signs of reviving interest in a thrust towards the East through Turkey. It was clear that great diplomatic pressure was being put on the Turks to provide France with favours and facilities which would help such an enterprise. Russia was still (in early 1807) Britain's ally, and held the Ionian islands, but could not be relied upon to support the Turks, with whom she had differences of her own. The villain of the piece was the French ambassador in Constantinople, Colonel Sebastiani, who was talking them into all kinds of concessions. The British government thought that a little judicious bullying might convince the Turks it would be safer to have no further dealings with the colonel. Consequently Admiral Duckworth was instructed to make a display of strength off Constantinople and, if possible, to provoke into a fight a Turkish squadron lying there.

The main problem was that Constantinople was at the far end of the Sea of Marmara, the entrance to which is through the narrow Dardanelles. To carry out his orders, Duckworth needed a 'soldier's wind', a wind blowing across the Dardanelles, which would be a fair wind both in and out. Such a wind was a long time coming, and while it was awaited the Turks had time to improve their defences. Eventually the wind came, and Duckworth reached Constantinople, where he cruised provocatively about. His orders were not to strike the first blow, but it was hoped that the Turkish squadron would attack, giving the opportunity for a punitive example to be made. The Turks, however, did not oblige with their ships, but opened up with shore-mounted guns which had been installed during the waiting period; these began to cause casualties. It was not part of Duckworth's orders to start a full-scale war, particularly when at a disadvantage. So in the end, all his squadron could do was to come out through the Dardanelles which, fortunately, the wind allowed it to do. It was no fault of Duckworth's, who was an able officer, but the whole episode brought little credit to anybody.

Also in 1807 came the second attack on Copenhagen. Once again the unfortunate Danes found themselves the centre of interest. The Treaty of Tilsit had been signed in June, effectively making Russia an ally of France, and among its provisions Russia conceded her interest in the Danish fleet. This could have been a catastrophe, as the gains of Trafalgar would be largely lost if the French made good their losses with Danish ships. The British government asked the Danes to hand over their fleet for safekeeping until the end of the war; the Danes refused. Therefore a fleet, under Admiral Lord Gambier, was sent to Copenhagen, and troops were landed to cut off the town on its inland side. Copenhagen was bombarded, and Denmark handed over her fleet. It was necessary, but nobody involved felt very happy about it.

In December 1807, Napoleon ordered ships in Brest, Lorient and Rochefort, to break the blockade and sail to Toulon. Admiral Ganteaume, who now commanded in Toulon, was ordered to leave port and join the ships from the Atlantic ports, as soon as they arrived. This was the beginning of another attempt by Napoleon to organise the movement of ships as if they were companies of men on the parade ground. His object was to eliminate the British from Sicily and Malta, where they were a steady threat to French activities on the Mediterranean coasts and could be an obstacle to any future operations in the Near East.

The proposed movements, though not quite on the scale of the preliminaries to Trafalgar, displayed a similar self-deception on the part of Napoleon. Once again he showed a supreme indifference to practicalities. The blockade of the Atlantic ports was not quite so intense as it had been, but it still proved impossible for the ships in Brest and Lorient to get out. The only vessels which did succeed in sailing were five ships of the line in Rochefort, under the stout-hearted Allemand. He succeeded in avoiding Admiral Strachan once again,

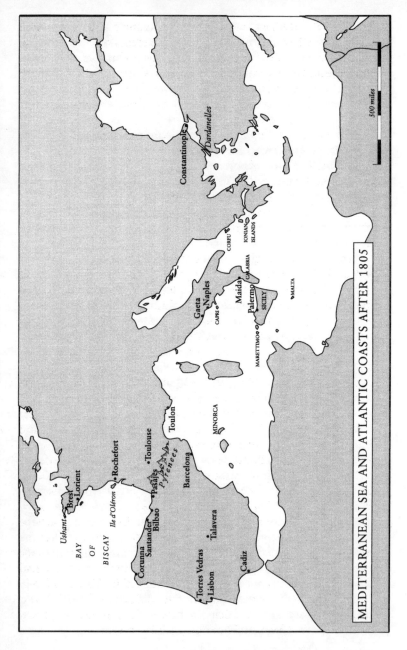

MEDITERRANEAN SEA AND ATLANTIC COASTS AFTER 1805

500 miles

Constantinople
Dardanelles

CORFU
IONIAN ISLANDS

CALABRIA
Gaeta
Naples
Maida
Palermo
CAPRI
SICILY
MARETTIMO
MALTA

Toulon
MINORCA

Toulouse
Rochefort
Pasajes
Pyrenees
Barcelona

Ushant
Brest
Lorient
Ile d'Oléron

BAY
OF
BISCAY

Corunna
Santander
Bilbao

Torres Vedras
Lisbon
Talavera

Cadiz

and reached the Mediterranean, where Ganteaume was to join him. Ganteaume's orders had, however, been changed. Instead of making straight for Sicily, where he might have arrived ahead of any British reinforcements, he was required to go first to Corfu. Corfu was under French occupation, and Ganteaume was to land additional troops there to counter any possible attack by the British. Only after this had been done, was he to attack Sicily.

It might have been expected that reinforcements would arrive in Sicily before Ganteaume got there via Corfu, and this is indeed what happened. As soon as Admiral Strachan discovered that Allemand had eluded him, he sailed to Cadiz. Learning from Admiral Purvis, blockading that port, that Allemand was not there, Strachan sailed on to Sicily. He finally made contact with Collingwood off Marettimo, at Sicily's western tip, bringing the total number of ships of the line there to fifteen.

Ganteaume had troubles besides the ships waiting to greet his arrival at Sicily. He left Toulon on 10 February 1808 and joined Allemand. This was not difficult; as Nelson had discovered, Toulon did not lend itself to a close blockade. The uncertain winds made it difficult to keep a fleet close inshore, and, from the hills behind Toulon, it was possible to see a fleet far out at sea. It was not difficult, therefore, for ships in the port to pick a suitable moment to come out. Frigates might lie close in to watch the direction they took, but, sooner or later, the frigates would have to report back to the blockading fleet, and contact with the escaping ships would be lost. In 1798 and 1805 the French had managed to leave port and get clear; they did so now but, like Nelson in 1798, ran into a violent storm, in which their fleet became scattered, and two of their three transports were lost. It was three weeks before the survivors re-assembled off Corfu. By this time Collingwood had been fully alerted to their presence in the eastern Mediterranean, and was searching for them south of Italy, while the main body of his fleet protected Sicily.

There were no options left to Ganteaume. His fleet was not as large as Napoleon had intended it to be, it had suffered badly from the weather, and he only had one out of three transports. Any faint hope that he might achieve something by a surprise attack on Sicily had been wrecked by his instructions to go first to Corfu. There was only one thing to do: he left what troops he had in Corfu and headed west keeping well to the south of Sicily and the waiting British ships. On 10 April he arrived back at Toulon, where he stayed.

Nothing had been achieved, and Napoleon had once again displayed his strange, almost wilful, lack of understanding of naval affairs. Ganteaume and Allemand were both competent and resourceful officers; allowed to use their judgement, and with better weather, they might have shaken the British hold on the Mediterranean. Napoleon's style of giving orders made sure that they did not.

Had Collingwood caught Ganteaume there would have been one more big sea battle. But little was lost. It was eighteen months before the French again set sail in any force, and then they were successfully contained by Collingwood's ships.

The most significant event of 1808 was the Spanish uprising, following Napoleon's imposition of his brother, Joseph, as King of Spain, and the removal of the rightful King Ferdinand III. This was to lead to the landing of British troops in Portugal, and the start of the Peninsular campaign. The British intervention was to show what the army could do, given proper basic military necessities and good generals, but success was not immediate. Credit is due to the government of the time for persisting with the enterprise in the face of initial setbacks. It could not have done so without command of the sea. This was now so well established that troops and supplies could be ferried to Spain (or, as will be seen, taken off) comparatively freely, and without serious threat from enemy vessels.

At first all went well. In August British troops landed on the Portuguese coast and after the battles of Rolica and Vimeiro the French evacuated Portugal. They did so under the terms of the Convention of Cintra, which allowed them to leave with all their spoils of war, and be taken back to France in British ships. The Convention was intensely unpopular at home, where it was thought that the French had been shamefully allowed to get away scot free after having been beaten. Nevertheless, it did establish British troops in Portugal, and it had one greatly advantageous result – although perhaps accidentally. The outcry against the Convention enforced the removal of two senior generals involved, so that command of the army in the peninsula eventually fell upon Sir Arthur Wellesley, soon to be Lord Wellington, later the Duke of Wellington.

In September before Wellesley's promotion, Sir John Moore led an army of 35,000 men into Spain. He was intended to co-operate with a Spanish army in northern Spain, to inflict a shattering defeat on the French. The whole enterprise ended in disaster; Moore found himself isolated, and about to be surrounded by greatly superior forces. The only thing he could do was to retreat across the mountains to Corunna (La Coruña), at the north-west corner of Spain. The retreat was a nightmare, and the army nearly fell apart, but it retained sufficient discipline and manhood to make a successful stand outside Corunna. Sir John Moore was killed, but the bulk of the army was given enough time to embark in the ships waiting for them. Not for the last time, a British army was saved by the navy's ability to mount a rescue operation on a hostile coast.

In spite of this disastrous reverse, British troops were still in south Portugal, and it was decided to persist with the military effort in the peninsula. In April 1809 Sir Arthur Wellesley, now in full command, landed again in Portugal. Neither he nor his soldiers saw England again for five years.

In Cadiz, Lord Collingwood had, with some difficulty, established a working relationship with the Spaniards. When the break with France came, the French ships in the harbour were dominated by shore-mounted guns, and had no alternative but to surrender. The Spaniards, therefore, had no urgent need of help from the British, and were inclined to be suspicious of them. They were, however, short of skilled men to work on the ships they had taken over and needed outside help. Gradually mutual confidence became established, Spain accepted British assistance in Cadiz, and Britain was granted base facilities in Minorca. Co-operation continued; a British garrison was established in Cadiz, which became a beach-head in French-occupied Spain for the rest of the war.

The Iberian peninsula became a theatre of war in which the two principal contestants had something like a balance of advantage. The French force was larger but it was operating among an intensely hostile population, and its supplies had to come by land. The Channel fleet blocked supply ships coming from ports in western France, and Collingwood threatened supplies from Mediterranean ports. Every item of equipment had to be slowly and painfully transported over appallingly bad roads under constant threat from Spanish guerrillas. The British army was comparatively small, but it had whatever assistance the inhabitants could give, and it was supplied, by sea, to whatever port was most convenient. So even was the balance that, for nearly four years, the fighting moved back and forth within Portugal and Spain; only at the end of that period did Wellesley, now Lord Wellington, riding across the border, bid a final farewell to Portugal and his army begin to move inexorably east.

Meanwhile, as well as making possible the war in Spain, the navy's task throughout the rest of the world continued. At about the time when Sir Arthur Wellesley's army was starting on its long task, the ever resourceful Admiral Allemand was about to make his presence felt again. With nine ships of the line, he escaped from Brest, and found protection from the blockading fleet some 200 miles south. His refuge was in the Aix Roads outside the port of Rochefort, waters he knew well. Off the coast of Rochefort is the Île d'Oléron, which shelters a stretch of water between itself and the mainland, rather as the Isle of Wight shelters the Solent and Spithead. The northerly part of the sheltered area is known as the Aix Roads, after the Île d'Aix in the entrance to it, and the southerly part of it is called the Basque Roads. What happened became known as the affair of the Aix Roads, or, sometimes, of the Basque Roads. It became a *cause célèbre*, and is still the source of strong feelings in historians, according to whether they incline to Admiral Lord Gambier or Captain Lord Cochrane. British ships of the line were not actively involved, but it is part of their story, because the point at issue was whether they should have been involved.

Allemand, with his nine ships of the line and five other ships, was anchored, in a strongly defensive position, within the roads. Superficially there is a resemblance to Admiral Brueys and his defensive position at the Nile; but only superficially, because Allemand's dispositions were very much more formidable and dangerous to attack. Also, of course, the waters were tidal. Britain could not afford to have a strong French fleet in a position from which it could easily get out, and which was difficult to blockade for long. Admiral Gambier, with eleven ships of the line, and a number of frigates and smaller craft, including fireships, had orders to attack and destroy it. Captain Lord Cochrane was in command of the frigates and smaller vessels. Under his energetic leadership a defensive boom was broken, and the fireships got among Allemand's fleet. To avoid them, Allemand's ships had to slip their anchors on a falling tide, and most of them ran aground. Cochrane frantically signalled to Gambier to send in the ships of the line, to destroy the French battleships before the tide rose again. Gambier, conscious of the dangers to big ships in the shoals and rocks of the roads, held back. As a result, most of the French were able to refloat on the next tide, and get to safety in the River Charente on which Rochefort lies.

Recriminations were bitter and Cochrane, after impassioned protests in Parliament, was broken and disgraced, ostensibly for dubious dealings on the Stock Exchange. He was reinstated many years later, but Britain lost the services of an undoubtedly able and venturesome officer for the remaining years of the war. Cochrane may not have been wholly right, but there is little doubt that a daring assault was not followed up as it should have been. Whatever else, it was not in the Nelson tradition.

Later in 1809 Collingwood directed what was to be his last action. He had received intelligence that Ganteaume, in Toulon, was preparing to sail, probably to Barcelona. In Spain, the erstwhile Sir Arthur Wellesley, now Lord Wellington, had fought a successful battle with the French at Talavera, and had retired to Portugal for the winter, behind the Lines of Torres Vedras. It was apparent to the French that he was not to be readily ejected, and that they must prepare for a hard campaign in the spring. Preparations would be enormously advanced if they could get a substantial convoy to Barcelona, by-passing the long hard road through the Pyrenees.

Collingwood moved to blockade Toulon and, once again, was up against the difficulty of maintaining a tight blockade on that port. He had many other tasks for his ships, and could not concentrate them all in one place for long; as has been seen, Toulon was not a port where the French could be bluffed into inactivity by one or two ships, as Duncan had bluffed the Dutch in the Texel. Seeing no immediate prospect of a move by the French, Collingwood had to withdraw to Minorca, now a British base by courtesy of Spain; there he could keep in some sort of touch with his other commitments in the Mediterranean, and still receive fairly up-to-date information, by frigate, about Ganteaume. Receiving a report that the French now really were about to leave, he took up station off the Spanish coast north-east of Barcelona. This time he was rewarded by the arrival of a frigate with the news that the French were leaving port and heading south-west. The report was exact, and the French fleet arrived; it was almost an anticlimax – there were twenty merchant vessels escorted by three ships of the line.

The French must have been relying on luck, which indeed they had enjoyed on previous occasions. Three ships were not, by any stretch of the imagination, enough to force a way through. Whatever had been hoped, this time there was no luck for them at all. The merchant ships were duly rounded up and Rear-Admiral Martin, with eight ships of the line, was sent to deal with the escort. The three ships of the escort, very sensibly, turned back to Toulon; but Martin caught up with them off the coast of Languedoc, where, as a last desperate defence, their crews ran them ashore.

This was almost Collingwood's last act in the Mediterranean; it also exemplifies what he was there for. Few of the activities of the Mediterranean fleet ended quite so neatly, but the frustration of French intentions was its major purpose. That Collingwood had succeeded was shown by the fact that, in spite of some setbacks to the British, there had been no successful French initiative in the Mediterranean during the four years since Trafalgar. It had called for constant vigilance and constant activity. Collingwood was not a young man, and the strain was too much. If ever a man deserved to enjoy a few years of peaceful retirement, he did, but all his requests for release were met with appeals to stay a little longer. He allowed duty to outweigh inclination once too often, and early in 1810 he died aboard the ship taking him home.

After 1810 the shooting war was, for the ships of the line, virtually over. Privateers were still active and there was plenty of action for the frigates and smaller craft. But, in all the ports of Europe, there was no fleet which could pose a serious threat to the Royal Navy, and, so long as vigilance was maintained, there never could be. Cruises and patrols by the big ships, to ram home the message, had to continue unabated but their function was, in practice, solely deterrence. In the Channel and North Sea, Lord Keith, now the C-in-C, maintained a watch on the commerce-raiding bases of northern France, and on developments in Antwerp and Ostend. In the Baltic, Sir James Saumarez commanded a fleet which seldom saw any action, but which kept trade routes open, and denied the use of that sea to Napoleon when he finally turned on Russia. The 'War of 1812' between the United States and Britain broke out in June 1812 and ended in December 1814; the naval engagements which took place were between frigates, not involving ships of the line.

Meanwhile, the principal British military activity was in Portugal and Spain. For three years the campaigning stayed fluid; at times Wellington's army attacked deep into Spain, at other times it was held fast within the borders of Portugal. In 1813 Wellington finally surged forward and retreated no more; in April 1814 he fought the last battle of the campaign at Toulouse.

Throughout this period the peninsular army and the Spanish guerrillas pinned down a large number of French troops (about half the number sent to Russia in 1812). So although from 1809 to 1813 the Peninsular war did not bring about any sudden dramatic change in the overall picture, its long-term effect was considerable. Not only was the British army slowly but surely getting the measure of the French, but Napoleon could not withdraw troops in any quantity from Spain to serve in north-east Europe; and, after the destruction of his army in Russia in 1812, he desperately needed experienced troops. Wellington was not only preparing to advance across the Pyrenees; he was making the task of the armies of Russia, Austria and Prussia in north-east Europe that much easier. The simultaneous advance, in 1813–14, of all the allied armies into France led to the abdication of Napoleon. Apart from the 'hundred days' between Napoleon's escape from Elba and the battle of Waterloo (which period did not heavily involve the navy), this was the end.

To sustain Wellington's campaign, every soldier, every article of equipment and all food or money to buy food, had to be transported by convoy across a thousand miles of potentially hostile ocean. This could be done because the Royal Navy commanded the sea. Wellington's supplies arrived regularly to whichever port was appropriate; French supplies had to come slowly and painfully over appalling roads, every mile subject to attack by the guerrillas.

Near the end of the Peninsular war, Wellington told Rear Admiral Martin, the second in command at Plymouth, 'If anyone wishes to know the history of this war, I will tell them that it is our maritime superiority gives me the power of maintaining my army while the enemy is unable to do so.' This says it all; throughout the period of the wars the navy had brought to a halt any French enterprise which involved sea crossings, frustrated all attempts to isolate Britain, and, by its support of Wellington's army in Spain, played a major part in the final physical occupation of Napoleon's territory.

Whether Napoleon was the monster he was thought to be in his time, or whether it might have been for the ultimate good of Europe if he had triumphed, is a question still argued by historians. What is certain is that no factor in his downfall can have been more important than the command of the sea, established by the Royal Navy's ships of the line. This was their last and greatest achievement.

Glossary of Nautical Terms

Abaft Nearer to the stern than . . .

Abeam In a direction roughly at right angles to the direction of sailing.

About To come about is to change from one tack to the other.

Aft Towards the rear or stern.

Ahead In the direction in which the ship is sailing.

Alongside Close to the side (rather than bow or stern) of the ship.

Amidships In the central part of the ship. Also: On the centre line of a ship or boat rather than to one side.

Athwart At right-angles to.

Athwartships At right angles across the fore-and-aft line of the ship.

Beam (i) The width of a ship or boat.
(ii) A structural member of the framing, which supports the deck planking.

Bear away To turn away from the direction from which the wind is coming.

Beat (to) (As in 'beat to windward') To make progress towards the direction from which the wind is coming by tacking (sailing from side to side).

Bilge The part of the hull below the lowest deck. Turn of the bilge: the curve where the bottom becomes the side.

Bitts Strongly mounted wooden framework to which anchor or mooring cables may be attached.

Boat Strictly, a small undecked vessel. Roughly, a vessel not large enough to be called a ship. (Ships are often wrongly referred to as boats, e.g., boat train.)

Boom (i) A spar at the foot of a sail.
(ii) A barrier formed by floating objects (e.g., barrels) linked by heavy rope or chain, strung across the mouth of a haven.

Bower anchor(s) The principal anchor(s) of a vessel. Normally stowed in the ship's bows.

Bow The forward part of a ship.

Bows The parts of the sides immediately adjacent to the foremost point of the ship (the stem). 'On the starboard bow' refers to something which may be seen by looking just to starboard of the stem.

Bowsprit A spar mounted in the fore part of the ship so that it projects over the foremost part of the ship (the stem).

Bulkhead An internal partition or 'wall' in the inside of a ship.

Buoy A conspicuous object (normally spherical, conical or cylindrical) anchored to the bottom and floating on the surface to mark the proximity of a hazard. For temporary purposes, anything which floats (e.g., a plank of wood) may be used as a buoy.

Cable (i) A strong heavy rope.

(ii) 200 yards, or one-tenth of a nautical mile.

Capstan A vertical winch, powered, in sailing days, by men pushing on capstan bars projecting radially from the top of the capstan (the drumhead).

Cat o' nine tails Nine cords, free for most of their length and plaited together at one end to form a handle. Used for inflicting punishment – flogging.

Centre The middle half or so of a line of ships, behind the 'van' and in front of the 'rear'.

Chains A narrow platform projecting from either side of a ship immediately behind (abaft) a mast. It was supported from below by ties to the hull and the shrouds of the mast were attached to its outside edge. By spreading their points of attachment further apart the platforms increased the stability the shrouds provided. The chains also formed a convenient point from which to cast the lead.

Close-hauled Sailing in a direction as near as possible to that from which the wind is coming.

Come about Change from one tack to another by turning through the direction of the wind.

Compressor A form of brake used on an anchor cable to control the rate at which it ran out.

Convoy A number of merchant ships sailing together in orderly formation and protected from enemy action by one or more naval ships.

Course The direction in which a ship is sailing expressed as a point of the compass. (In modern times the direction is expressed in degrees.)

Dead ahead In precisely the direction in which the ship is sailing.

Deadeyes Thick discs of wood, each having three holes, always used in pairs. One would be attached to the bottom of a shroud and the other to the chains or other fixed point. Small-diameter rope (lanyards) passed through the holes enabled the two to be pulled together to tension the shroud. Their operation was exactly like that of two triple-pulley blocks.

Dead reckoning Keeping track of one's progress by marking one's direction and estimated distance travelled (based on measured speed) on a chart, as opposed to finding one's position by astral navigation.

Draught The minimum depth of water in which a ship can technically float.

Fathom Six feet (1.8288 metres).

Fair wind A wind enabling one to sail in the direction required without tacking.

Fleet Usually, a substantial number of ships under one command sailing together.

Fore Prefix used with nouns to indicate that they relate to the forward part of the vessel.

Forecastle Originally a structure or 'castle' at the front end of a ship from which weapons could be fired. In a ship of the line, the decked area around the foremast. Now, the accommodation immediately below the foredeck.

Foremast The foremost mast of a ship having two or more masts. (In a small vessel, a ketch or a yawl, it may also be the mainmast.)

Footrope A rope, hung horizontally below a yard, on which the topmen stood when handling the sail.

Fother To manoeuvre a sail or piece of canvas over a hole in the side to reduce the inflow of water.

Forward Towards the bow of the ship.

Frames Heavy timber structures set up along the keel, like ribs, to which the planking was fastened.

Gybe When wearing a vessel there is a moment when any fore-and-aft sail has to swing from one side to the other with the wind behind it. This action is to gybe. In a small vessel with a boomed mainsail, in a fresh wind, this can be a dangerous operation unless skilfully carried out.

Gundeck The deck on which the main armament of a ship was carried. Ships of the line were known as two-deckers or three-deckers according to the number of decks on which guns were carried.

Halliard, Halyard A rope used to haul a yard or sail up a mast.

Haul wind (to) To turn nearer to the direction from which the wind is coming.

Hawshole An opening in the bow planking through which the anchor cable passes.

Heads Ship's lavatories, in sailing ships normally sited forward.

Head wind An adverse wind, blowing from the direction in which it is wished to sail.

Heave to Set the sails and rudder of a vessel so that she makes no headway.

Helm A word used in various ways connected with steering, e.g., helm orders, at the helm, helmsman, etc.

Hoist (to) The operation of hauling something up.

Hold The lowest compartment in a ship. Has a varying connotation according to the type of ship, e.g., in a merchant ship a hold may extend from the keel to the uppermost deck.

In irons A vessel is said to be 'in irons' when, having failed to come about, she lies still in the water, drifting slowly to leeward.

Jib-boom A spar fastened to and forming a continuation of the bowsprit.

Kedge anchor An anchor smaller than the bower, normally used in harbour manoeuvres in calm weather.

Knees Bracket-shaped pieces of timber strengthening the corner of a frame.

Knot One nautical mile (1.14 land miles) per hour. The expression 'knots per hour' sometimes heard (even from seamen) is incorrect.

Landfall The first sight of land at the end of a voyage.

Lanyard A short length of small-diameter rope used in handling or controlling items of equipment (see 'deadeyes').

Larboard Old form of 'port'. The left-hand side (facing forward) of a vessel.

Lashing Small-diameter length of rope used to fasten two things together.

Latitude Distance north or south of the Equator, expressed in degrees.

Lead line Line with lead weight on one end, used to measure depth of water.

Lee Area sheltered from the wind.

Lee shore A coastline towards which the wind is blowing.

Leeward In the direction towards which the wind is blowing.

Leeway Sideways movement in the direction of the wind made by a ship sailing across the wind.

Line of bearing Ships moving forward alongside each other.

Line of battle Ships in single file (line ahead).

Log book (or Log) Daily record of ship's activities kept by the captain and/or the master of a vessel.

Longitude Distance east or west of the Greenwich meridian, expressed in degrees.

Luff (i) The windward edge of a sail.

(ii) To alter course into the wind.

Mainmast The principal mast of a vessel with more than one mast.

Mast A vertical spar. In big sailing ships, mast was a generic term referring to a complex structure embodying a lower mast, topmast, and topgallant mast.

Mizzen-mast Generally, the aftermost mast of a vessel with more than one mast. (However, the aftermost mast is not always called the mizzen, e.g., in a schooner the aftermost of the two masts is the mainmast.)

Orlop deck The lowest deck in a ship.

Planking The outer skin of a wooden ship or boat.

Poop deck A short deck raised above the quarterdeck at the aft end of a ship.

Port (i) The left-hand side (facing forward) of a ship or boat. 'Port' superseded the term 'larboard' during the first half of the nineteenth century.

(ii) A coastal town having a haven and facilities for shipping.

Press The system of taking men by force to serve in the navy. It was carried out by 'press gangs', squads of reliable seamen under a junior officer who roamed the streets of seaports seeking men to impress.

Privateer A privately owned vessel, licensed by a government to carry out warlike acts – usually against merchant ships.

Quarterdeck In a ship of the line, the part of the open deck abaft the mainmast. The command centre of the ship.

Ratlines Horizontal ropes fastened to the shrouds forming steps or rungs up which the crew could climb.

Reach (to) To sail approximately at right angles to the wind. For most sailing vessels a comparatively easy course to maintain.

Rear In a line of ships the last few ships in the line, perhaps a fifth or a quarter of the total number.

Rigging The system of ropes supporting the masts and controlling the sails. Fixed supporting ropes are 'standing rigging' and ropes controlling sails are 'running rigging'.

Run (to) To sail in approximately the same direction as the wind.

Sheet A rope controlling a sail.

Sheet anchor Anchor carried as security in case needed as well as the bower anchor(s).

Ship Strictly, a large, three-masted vessel, square-rigged on all three masts. As generally used, a substantial sea-going vessel.

Shoal Shallow water in which a ship might risk grounding.

Shrouds System of ropes supporting a mast laterally (roughly athwartships).

Sling (to) To support something by suspending it on ropes from a fixed structure.

Soldier's wind A wind enabling a vessel to reach. Used particularly in connection with fairly short distances when a soldier's wind serves equally well going and coming back.

Spring A rope, other than the main cable, attached to an anchor so that, by hauling on it the angle at which the ship lies to the wind or tide can be altered.

Squadron A number of ships, less than a fleet, under the command of one senior officer. Several squadrons might form a fleet under a senior admiral.

Square sail A four-sided sail suspended from a spar. Usually trapezoidal rather than square.

Stay A rope supporting a mast on a fore-and-aft line (or nearly so in the case of a backstay).

Staysail A triangular sail hung from a stay.

Starboard The right-hand side (facing forward) of a vessel.

Stem The foremost part of the bows.

Stempost The foremost structural member to which plank ends are fastened.

Stern The rear end of a vessel.

Strike (to) To show surrender to an opposing ship by taking down, or striking, the national colours.

Swell Long, unbreaking waves at sea.

Tack (to) To change direction of a vessel by turning through the direction of the wind. A sailing vessel is said to be 'on the starboard tack' when the wind is coming over the starboard side, and 'on the port (or larboard) tack' when the wind is coming over the port (or larboard) side.

Tackle A system of ropes and pulley blocks to give mechanical advantage when handling a load.

Tiller A bar attached to the top of the rudder by which a vessel can be steered, either by direct handling or, via ropes or mechanisms, by a wheel.

Transom The flat part of the stern of a vessel.

Van The front few ships of a line of ships, perhaps a fifth or a quarter of the total number.

Waterline The line round a ship formed by the surface of the water in which it is floating.

Wear (to) To change from one tack to the other by turning away from the direction of the wind.

Weather gage Upwind of opponent, therefore able to close and attack at will.

Western Approaches The area of sea to the south-west of the British Isles forming the approach to the English Channel and the Irish Sea.

Winch A mechanical device for hauling on a rope by winding it round a drum. Mechanical advantage is provided by the radial length of the winding handles and possibly by gearing.

Yard A spar, crossing the mast of a ship, from which a sail is suspended.

Yardarm The outer end of a yard.

Bibliography

Beresford, Rear-Admiral Lord Charles, and Wilson H. W., *Nelson and his Times* (Harmsworth Bros, 1897)

Boudriot, Jean (trans D. H. Roberts), *The 74 Gun Ship* Vol. iv (4 vols, Jean Boudriot, 1988)

Bradford, Ernle, *Nelson, The Essential Hero* (Granada, 1979)

'A British Seaman', *Life Aboard a Man of War* (Blackie Fullerton & Co, 1829)

Bryant, Arthur, *The Years of Endurance* (Collins, 7th edn, 1951)

Bryant, Arthur, *Years of Victory* (Collins, 3rd edn, 1951)

Bryant, Arthur, *The Age of Elegance* (Collins, 1950)

Bryant, Arthur, *The Fire and The Rose* (Collins, 1965)

Byrn, John D. Jnr, *Crime and Punishment in the Royal Navy* (Scolar Press, 1989)

Chandler, David, *Napoleon* (Weidenfeld & Nicolson, 1973)

Chatterton, E. Keble, *The Story of the British Navy* (Mills & Boon, 1911)

Churchill, T. O., *Life of Lord Viscount Nelson* (T. Bensley, 1808)

Clarke, Rev. James Stainier, and M'Arthur, John, *Life of Admiral Lord Nelson K.B.* (2 vols, Cadell, 1809)

Douglas, General Sir Howard, *A Treatise on Naval Gunnery* (Conway Maritime Press, 1982; first publ. 1820)

Dugan, James, *The Great Mutiny* (André Deutsch, 1966)

Forrester, C. S., *Lord Nelson* (Bobbs Merril Co, Indianapolis, 1929)

Fremantle, Anne, ed, *The Wynne Diaries*, Vol. iii (3 vols, Oxford University Press, 1935–40)

Gardiner, Leslie, *The British Admiralty* (Blackwood & Sons, 1968)

Gardner, John, *Warships of the Royal Navy*, 1st Series – *Sail* (Hugh Evelyn, 1968)

Glover, Michael, *Warfare in the Age of Napoleon* (Cassell, 1980)

Hart, Roger, *England Expects* (Wayland Ltd, 1972)

Henderson, James, *The Frigates* (Adlard Coles, 1970)

Henderson, James, *Sloops and Brigs* (Adlard Coles, 1972)

Hogg, Ian, and Batchelor, John, *The Naval Gun* (Blandford Press, 1978)

Holland, A. J., *Ships of British Oak* (David & Co, 1971)

Howarth, David, *Trafalgar, The Nelson Touch* (Collins, 1961)

Huggett, Frank E., *Life and Work at Sea* (Harrap, 1975)

Jenkins, E. H., *A History of the French Navy* (Macdonald & Co, 1973)

Johnson, William, *History of the Mutiny at Spithead* (Thomas Tegg, 1842)

Keegan, John, *The Price of Admiralty* (Hutchinson, 1988)

Kemp, Peter, *History of the Royal Navy* (A. Barker, 1969)

Kemp, Peter, ed, *The Oxford Companion to Ships and the Sea* (Oxford University Press, 1988)

Kennedy, Ludovic, *Nelson and his Captains* (Collins, 1975)

Lavery, Brian, *The Ship of the Line* (2 vols, Conway Maritime Press Ltd, 1983–4)

Lavery, Brian, *The 74 Gun Ship 'Bellona'* (Conway Maritime Press Ltd, 1985)

Lavery, Brian, *Nelson's Navy* (Conway Maritime Press Ltd, 1989)

Lloyd, Christopher, *St Vincent and Camperdown* (Batsford, 1963)

Lloyd, Christopher, *The British Seaman* (Collins, 1968)

Lloyd, Christopher, *The Nile Campaign* (David & Charles, 1973)

Lloyd, Christopher, *Nelson and Sea Power* (English Universities Press, 1973)

Mackesy, Piers, *The War in the Mediterranean* (Longman, 1957)

Mahan, Captain A. T., *The Influence of Sea Power on the French Revolution and Empire* (Sampson, Low, Marston, Searle & Rivington, 1892)

Mahan, Captain A. T., *The Influence of Sea Power on History 1660–1783* (Sampson, Low, Marston, Searle & Rivington, 1897)

Moore, Sir Alan, *Sailing Ships of War* (Halton, 1926)

Naval Chronical Vols 1–6

Navy Records Society, *Logs of the Great Sea Fights 1 & 2*

—*The Keith Papers*

—*The Saumarez Papers*

—*Nelson's Letters to his Wife*

—*The Fighting Instructions*

Nicolas, Sir Nicholas Harris, ed, *Dispatches and Letters of Vice-Admiral Lord Viscount Nelson* (7 vols, Henry Colburn, 1844–6)

Oman, Carola, *Nelson* (Hodder & Stoughton, 1947)

Padfield, Peter, *Guns at Sea* (Hugh Evelyn, 1973)

Parkinson, C. Northcote, *War in the Eastern Seas 1793–1815* (George Allen & Unwin, 1954)

Pope, Dudley, *The Black Ship* (Weidenfeld & Nicolson, 1963)

Pope, Dudley, *The Great Gamble* (Weidenfeld & Nicolson, 1972)

Pope, Dudley, *Life in Nelson's Navy* (George Allen & Unwin, 1981)

Public Record Office	ADM 52 3223/3	Master's Log, *Minerve*
	3526	Master's Log, *Victory*
—ADM 51 1187/3		Captain's Log, *Victory*
	1482	Captain's Log, *Victory*
—ADM 52 3711/2		Master's Log, *Victory*
—ADM 51 2776		Captain's Log, *Revenge*
—ADM 52 3524/13		Master's Log, *Veteran*
—ADM 3 126		Board Minutes, March/May 1801
—ADM 50 65		Sir Hyde Parker's Journal
—ADM 50 93		Sir John Jervis's Journal
—ADM 12 26/6		Courts Martial Digest 55–06
—ADM 2 1121		Courts Martial Details
—ADM 13 103		Courts Martial Details

Rodger, N. A. M., *The Wooden World* (Collins, 1968)

Shankland, Peter, *Beware of Heroes* (W. M. Kimber, 1975)

Society for Nautical Research, *Mariner's Mirror*, Vol. 73, November 1987, Ole Feldbaek, 'Humanity or Ruse de Guerre'

Stuart Jones, Commander E. H., (RN), *An Invasion that Failed* (Basil Blackwell, 1950)

Tucker, Jedediah Stephens, *Memoirs of the Rt. Hon. The Earl of St Vincent* (Richard Bentley, 1844)

Tute, Warren, *The True Glory* (Macdonald & Co, 1983)

Southey, Robert, *The Life of Nelson*, with an introduction by Henry Newbolt (Constable & Co, 1916)

Wheeler, W., *The Letters of Private Wheeler*, ed Captain B. H. Liddell Hart (Michael Joseph, 1951)

Whipple, A. B. C., *Fighting Sail* (Time & Life Books, 1978)

Index